Hospice Plain and Simple

The Essential Guide to Death and Dying

BRENDA HAMPTON, RN

White Shoe Press

CONTENTS

INTRODUCTION

This book is for everyone! Patients, their families and caregivers will benefit from the information contained between the covers of this book. Whether you're the patient or making decisions for a loved one, you'll find extremely useful and direct information with loads of resources to follow up on your own. You may not need it all right now, but it's very helpful to have this type of information well ahead of the time when you truly need it.

Primarily I'll be speaking to the person who is the patient, but there are times I will talk to the family members and caregivers. All information is useful for everyone.

My goals for this book are to give you direction, support about a scary topic, a good understanding of what hospice is and isn't, and how you can access it for free. Yes, *free*. You've paid for hospice all your working life, and it's a Medicare benefit you have a right to and deserve.

Consider me, a very experienced hospice nurse, with over 27 years of experience, your tour guide through a process you've never been through. When you need expertise for something you don't know how to do, you hire an expert, right? Well, hospice and hospice nurses are the experts on death and dying, and having hospice walk with you on this path will be helpful to you in more ways than you can imagine right now.

For simplicity, I'll refer to all forms of end-of-life care, palliative care and comfort care, as hospice.

I'll be using words like death and dying, terminal illness, cancer, and other direct words. Most people want straight talk, and in this book, you'll receive it. Not unkindly, but in a manner that won't leave you wondering what's going to happen next.

I'm going to show you what dying looks like and how you or your loved one can have a better, non-scary, death.

So, let's get to it.

CHAPTER I

THE SHORT DESCRIPTION

The Short Description

Hospice is a care program, not a place, covered 100% by Medicare, Medicaid, or other insurance for people diagnosed with a terminal illness and expected to die within six months from that disease. (Not from the time of diagnosis, but from the time hospice evaluates the person, if left untreated.) Hospice is also designed for people to die at home where they are most comfortable and cared for by the people they are most comfortable with- their family.

Let's move on to an in-depth description of the program, then later I'll break things down, so you'll understand how your disease generally progresses.

CHAPTER 2

THE NITTY GRITTY

What is hospice? Exactly.

You might have heard the word before spoken in hushed whispers of a back bedroom or around a kitchen table late at night after the children have gone to bed when grandma wasn't doing too well. I'm going to bring this word, and everything associated with it out into the light so you can see and understand why people do the things they do when they're dying.

Hospice not a secret.

It's not taboo.

It's not a way to kill people.

It's a way to care for people who are dying in a dignified, respectful way, and *reduces fear* from the death process for everyone.

You may have ideas of what the dying process and death look like based on movies or TV portrayals, but I assure you those dramatic interpretations are not usually the case. Most deaths are quiet, with a pattern of changes that are predictable as the body winds down and ceases to function. Kind of like a car running out of gas. We'll get to all those details soon, so you'll have a much better understanding.

Hospice is a philosophy developed by Dame Cicely Saunders in 1967 including palliative care, end-of-life care or comfort care.

Since then, hospice care as a philosophy, an organization, and care model has evolved and grown worldwide from its origins in England. Of course, people of all cultures have cared for their sick and dying since the beginning of humanity, but without the understanding of how and why things happen, how to prepare for those changes, and needed support after those changes have ended.

Everything explained about the Medicare guidelines in this book is current as of the publication date.

Hospice is also an approach to health and healthcare that doesn't hurry or slow down the dying process.

Take a minute to reread that last sentence and think about what it means. We don't slow down the dying process, but neither do we speed it up. We keep you comfortable and let Mother Nature take its course without interference.

If curative treatments make you so sick that you want to die, then it's time for hospice.

If you're unable to get to your treatments any longer, it's time for hospice.

Hospice is covered 100% by Medicare. Yes, 100%. (You don't get that deal with anything anymore.) Whatever hospice covers, they cover 100%. If they don't cover it, it's not covered at all and it's an out-of-pocket cost.

Most traditional insurance programs have a cap on how much money they will pay for hospice care, but most plans have some hospice coverage. If you're not on Medicare or

Medicaid, but private insurance, ensure what policy you choose has hospice coverage.

Those are lots of benefits to you, but you may be asking yourself: what do I have to give up to get the service you're talking about?

It's A Change in Thinking, It's Not Giving Up

LET me explain this a bit more.

You absolutely can have curative treatment OR you can have comfort care/hospice and Medicare will pay for both of them, *but not at the same time.*

You do have to pick one or the other. Each is a different philosophy in opposition to the other. You can't put your foot on the brake and the gas at the same time and expect to get anywhere, can you? It's the same principle here.

The reason you don't go to any appointments outside of hospice is that all of the billing (money) goes to hospice for your care and needs on that program. If you go to your PCP or regular doctor they won't get paid by Medicare. It's as simple as billing.

Remember: Medicare and Medicaid pay 100% for hospice care.

Once you join a hospice program you no longer see your primary care provider (PCP) or go to any medical appointments. The reason is that the hospice doctor becomes your doctor and will handle all aspects of your care. You won't be going to any treatments, appointments or further procedures outside of hospice.

In the situation that you fall and break a hip that

requires surgery to fix it, Medicare will cover that. Hospice will help you and your family negotiate the details of that process.

There are rare occasions where hospice will consent to, and pay for, a few radiation treatments for pain control. What that means is that sometimes a tumor can press on a nerve and no matter how much medication we give the patient the pain is still not controlled. This is called *therapeutic radiation* for pain control only.

Once you choose comfort care, then it's the time to cancel any other appointments you may have previously set up. If you've just gotten out of the hospital, there may be appointments set up for you by the hospital staff. Cancel them. You should also call your primary care provider, or doctor, and let them know you've selected hospice. Many people have long relationships with their doctors, so it's nice to be able to say goodbye to the person who has been your healthcare provider. Your primary doctor can't fulfill all of your needs on hospice and your care will be transferred to the hospice medical director.

You will no longer call 911 for emergency needs.

THAT SOUNDS SCARY, I know, and there are a few exceptions to this firm rule. If you fall and you've got bones hanging out, that's a 911 call. Then call hospice afterward.

Hospice is not an emergency service, but it is a 24-hour service and there is a difference between those. We don't want your family to call 911 when you're dying, on hospice and it's expected.

If you fall, have no injuries and just can't get up, you, or your caregiver, will need to call hospice. They will send a nurse to help you off the floor and assess for any injuries. This way we keep you out of the hospital. That's one of the biggest goals of hospice, to keep you at home and safe. If the hospice nurse can't get you up, then they will call for some extra muscle from the fire department, but it's not a 911 call.

- If you have trouble breathing, you call hospice.
- If you feel like you're developing a bladder infection, you call hospice.
- If you don't understand something and have questions, you call hospice.

CHAPTER 3

THE GENERAL GUIDELINES

T his next section goes over the general guidelines about how a person becomes eligible for hospice, what hospice does, what it doesn't do, what it provides, and how you can request an evaluation for yourself or a loved one.

An evaluation of your condition is always good information because it provides a baseline (starting point) about how close you are to needing or qualifying for hospice.

You must be at a certain declined level in your disease to qualify for hospice care. The hospice nurse who evaluates you will give you useful information to make decisions about your life, what kind of care you want, or don't want, and what kind of death you want to experience: letting Mother Nature take its course, or in the hospital with full-court press.

Those are the only two choices. Stop or go. There is no in-between.

Getting handed a terminal diagnosis doesn't mean immediate death.

There are a lot of things that happen between diagnosis

and death, and this book will help you understand what they are and how to handle them.

IMPORTANT POINTS: #1

There's a lot of living to do before the dying time comes. Remember that. Read that again.

If you've been waiting to do something, don't wait any longer. Do it *now*. That's advice for anyone at any time in their life: don't wait. People in the prime of their lives get killed every day in car accidents they never expected, and tomorrow isn't promised.

Take that time, no matter how long it is, and do something awesome with it.

- Go on that trip you've always wanted to take.
- Go see the grandkids.
- Catch up with friends.
- Forgive the grudge you've been holding for too many years.
- Make peace with life.

WITH ANY HOSPICE diagnosis the hospice doctor needs to be able to tell Medicare yes, without any further intervention you have approximately six months or less to live, given the natural course of disease process. That's the Medicare lingo.

To qualify for hospice, the diagnosis must be terminal, which means there is no cure. There may be treatment, but no cure. And the *treatment must be stopped prior* to going to hospice.

The prognosis-the estimate of how much time someone has left to live-must be within the six-month timeframe hospice requires.

Or no further life-sustaining/life-prolonging treatment is available or desired. That means *you voluntarily stop treatment.* Some people make the decision to have limited treatment, or even no treatment, should they develop cancer or other life-limiting disease.

Examples of treatments are:

- Chemotherapy
- Radiation therapy
- Surgery for cancer that has ended with no improvement in your condition
- Or you're unable to tolerate any of the above treatments.

IMPORTANT POINTS #2

You *must be in decline* to qualify for hospice. Some diagnoses, though terminal, can still take years to get to the truly dying phase.

Examples of those would be:

- Alzheimer's Disease
- Dementia
- Congestive Heart Failure
- COPD/Emphysema
- Lou Gehrig's Disease (ALS)
- Parkinson's Disease

All are long-term and chronic, requiring long-term, or

custodial care, but are not immediately terminal and *not yet appropriate* for hospice care.

If curative treatment ends in remission, then you don't qualify for, or even need, hospice. That's great!

Remission means the disease is not growing, not changing, not getting worse and the person's condition is stable or even improved. How long someone remains in remission is always a guessing game but can go on for many years.

Those are the general guidelines for hospice, no matter what the diagnosis is.

IMPORTANT POINTS #3:

- Hospice is free.
- You must qualify for it.
- Six months or less to live.
- Support for your family after you die.
- Hospice isn't for everyone.

What if You Live Longer Than Six Months?

If you live for six months and one day you aren't kicked off hospice because you've lived too long! Behind the scenes, your hospice nurse continually evaluates you at every visit for an ongoing need to have hospice care because your condition is still terminal, though it may be slower than first estimated.

When you come onto a hospice program you're brought on for two 90-day certification periods. After that, you're re-certified for unlimited 60-day increments until your death or become so stable you are no longer dying. In that case you'll be discharged from hospice for what is termed: extended diagnosis.

We like to call it *graduating from hospice*. That's a great thing.

At a later time, you can come back to hospice when your condition is again in a downward trajectory. There is no limit to how many times you can do this. I personally took care of a woman with liver cancer who came into our in-patient hospice unit to die *four times*. That sounds pretty crazy, doesn't it? The first three times she went home for few months. She evidently had something significant she wanted to live for, or had to resolve, before she could move on. On the fourth time to our unit, she finally was able to let go and passed peacefully.

Behind the scenes the hospice staff are always documenting, with every visit, the decline they see in you with things that can be measured. This includes weight loss, clothing size change, appetite loss, vital sign changes, loss of interest in activities you previously had been engaged in, and a continued decline that may also include sleeping more, sometimes up 24 hours a day.

If you become stable, your hospice must follow the Medicare guidelines and prepare you for discharge from hospice services.

Sometimes, when someone gets more care from health-care providers, has safety adjustments made to their home, and their medications well-managed, people do improve.

There's good and bad news about that. The good news is: you're actually improved from when you were in serious decline. The bad news is: you no longer qualify for hospice care!

Your feelings about that can be conflicted, and that's

expected. You can't change the rules, but you can change how you feel about them.

What Happens If You No Longer Qualify for Hospice?

Hospice will give you some time to get adjusted to the idea, generally two weeks. They'll prepare you and your family for the upcoming end of hospice service. You'll get a written notice, the ability to protest the discharge directly to Medicare, and your nurse will talk to you about it.

Graduating from hospice happens more often with people who have non-cancer diagnoses, such as those long-term diseases I mentioned before: Alzheimer's Disease, Parkinson's Disease and many more.

You'll be given a timeframe for when the last visit will be, and you'll generally have your medications refilled for two weeks. Your medical equipment will be changed out, and Medicare will pay what they previously paid for.

Then, you go back to doing things as you did prior to hospice, so you may want to make appointments soon.

You'll return to going to your primary doctor or care provider and return to paying the co-pays for them.

You'll get your prescriptions where you previously got them.

Any medical equipment you will continue to need will be billed to your insurance or Medicare, as it was previously. It just needs to be set up again and hospice will do that.

If you still need some help at home, you may be able to have Palliative Care service, or Home Healthcare referrals. Those services have different guidelines and are outside the scope of this book.

Hospice will be able to make referrals to those areas if you need them and they're appropriate.

On the other side of the 6-month rule, people do remain on hospice service for longer than the six-month estimate. The reason for this is that some people have a slower trajectory than initially estimated.

That's okay. Everyone's journey is different.

The thing to keep in mind is that with every visit the nurse makes with you, he/she will be documenting measurable changes they see in your condition. Sometimes cancers grow more slowly than anticipated. Sometimes there are factors we just can't measure, such as the desire of someone to live, or their desire to die. Regardless, if you're in continued decline, you'll continue to receive hospice care.

CHAPTER 4

HOW MUCH TIME DO YOU HAVE LEFT?

One of the most frequent questions I'm asked is how much time someone has to live. Both patients and families ask that question, because it affects so many aspects of life.

Hospice nurses develop a sense of when a person is dying. That's never written in stone, but the nurse will be able to give you an idea of the changes and decline they see in you.

One of the hospice doctors I used to work with gave me the best way of estimating how much time someone has left.

Think back and remember how you were *about six months ago*: what you were doing, eating, activity, pain, sleep, all of it. Then compare that to how you were *six weeks ago*.

Compare that to *now*.

What are the changes you can identify during those time periods?

That will give you a rough idea of the speed of your changes and the probable speed of the changes coming up.

Hospice never gives definite timeframes when someone is dying, because there are too many factors which influence the dying process to account for.

Many times, families will cling to the timeframe given and get upset if their loved one does, or doesn't, pass away in that timeframe given. We aren't psychics and have no clear way to look to the future, but we can give a rough estimate.

Outside of a sudden event, a heart attack, stroke or something unforeseen and catastrophic, there is usually a decline of some sort before someone is actually dying.

You generally don't just poof, die. Especially if there isn't a significant disease process responsible for the changes.

You may have high blood pressure, poor kidney function, weight loss, diabetes, poor eyesight and fallen eighteen times in the last week, but you aren't dying from any single one of those illnesses. All together, they are certainly contributing to your decline, but you can be very stable in this declined state for months or even years.

People generally decline in one of two ways:

A long slow, or very slow way, over many, many months.

Or they decline in a big chunk.

An example would be someone who is slowly winding down. You know they're going to stop at some point, but you don't know when. You can see the wobbles and know the end is coming, but they haven't stopped yet.

Chunk decline is going from independent in walking, to needing a walker, to needing a wheelchair, to becoming bedbound, and each change seems very sudden.

People decline in one way or the other. Have a look at yourself and recall how you were doing six months ago, compare that to six weeks ago and compare to now.

Are you the long, slow decliner, or a chunker? (Those are my terms, not official hospice terms.)

Neither one is better nor worse than the other. It's just a way to look at how someone, maybe you, has been making their changes and are likely to continue to change in the same way in the future.

CHAPTER 5

DO YOU HAVE TO HAVE HOSPICE?

One last question you may be pondering. What if you accept hospice service and don't like it? Or you don't like your nurse? Or don't like having people in your home despite the benefit? People who are very private, or very controlling personalities, have the hardest time with this.

Hospice is an optional service you've paid for all your life by paying into Medicare. If you don't use it, the benefit (and all the money you paid into the system) goes to waste. You can't give it away. No one else can use it except you.

But you definitely don't have to have this service.

If you qualify for hospice, you are strongly encouraged to at least try it out. Kinda like eating a new vegetable for the first time. You're not sure it looks good, you're suspicious, but everyone is telling you it's good for you, it smells kinda funny, but in the end after you try it you absolutely love it!

A good reason, and maybe the best reason, to accept hospice, is that your loved ones will have extra help while you're dying and grief support, often termed bereavement, for a year after you die.

Grief support is also free to them. They can use it as much or as little as they need, but it's there for a year. Some families don't need grief support. Other people might need it on occasion and some families need it before their loved one dies. There are a lot of factors to grief, and I'll go into some of them later.

People do sign off hospice service. The most common reason is that they want one more last try at curative, life-prolonging treatment, like surgery, chemo or radiation.

Remember: you can have these treatments, and you can have hospice service, but not at the same time. One is curative and one is comfort. Medicare will pay for both, but only one at a time.

If you want to sign off of hospice, that's okay and always your decision. Hospice would really like you to be ready emotionally for hospice and have all the curative treatments over with before you agree to hospice service, but it happens.

The good part is that the process to leave hospice is simple.

You sign a piece of paper that says you *revoke hospice service*. The moment you sign the paper hospice service ends. There is no waiting period. You can still return to hospice service, if you wish, when the time is right for you.

Please don't wait until you're taking your last breath.

Waiting too long benefits nobody.

IMPORTANT POINTS #4:

- You don't have to die in six months.

- Sometimes people graduate from hospice.
- Decline is long and slow, or fast and in big chunks.
- Hospice isn't for everyone.

SUMMARY OF SECTION ONE:

- You've been given a terminal diagnosis.
- You've completed all curative or life-prolonging treatments.
- You've made the decision to accept the hospice philosophy.
- You've been signed up/admitted to a hospice program in your home.

CHAPTER 6

THE GUIDELINES

HOSPICE IN GREATER DETAIL

Everything hospice does and provides has a guideline written by Medicare. Every hospice must follow the same guidelines that are updated every few years. You won't get more, or better, things with one hospice over another, and that applies to not-for-profit hospices as well as for-profit hospices.

If you talk to a representative from hospice about what they offer but want to shop around and call another hospice to compare them, they will tell you the same thing. You have the right to choose any hospice you like, but they all follow the same guidelines provided by Medicare.

You're free to choose any hospice you wish. Some assisted living centers, or private care homes, prefer to work with certain hospices. If you don't agree to use the hospice they prefer, then you may be forced to move if you strongly want to use a different hospice. If you don't care all that much and want to stay in the facility you're in, then no worries. Use the hospice your facility likes. (I don't know how legal that is according to hospice guidelines, but that's outside the scope of this book).

How To Find A Hospice

Here is a link where you can search for a hospice by state.

You can also search CMC (Center for Medicare and Medicaid Services) It's pretty boring but gives you information how the hospice you're looking at has been rated in the past. Remember that no hospice is perfect, but a pretty good score is good enough for most people and situations. for public scoring and analysis by families.

CHAPTER 7

HOSPICE GOES WHERE YOU LIVE

This includes independent living, which is a house or apartment, assisted living, or if you live in the home of a friend or relative. When you, or your loved one, are going into a care center, make sure they can handle the care needed when you're at end-of-life.

Some facilities will make you move to another care center when you require more care than they want to, or can, provide. Other care centers (like the ones that include independent care, assisted living and long-term care all in one facility) will charge you for every additional service, which can be quite costly on top of everything else you're already paying for there. Make sure you understand their rules.

If you're unhappy with the hospice you signed on with, you have the right to change hospices once every certification period. **Reminder:** that's initially 2–90-day periods, and then in 60-day increments, or certification periods, after that.

Hospice does not replace the family, or a hired caregiver

as the 24-hour presence in the home to perform all the daily and moment-to-moment tasks needed by someone who is unable to care for themselves. Cooking, feeding, laundry, bathing, and giving medications, which can include narcotics.

CHAPTER 8

IMPORTANT REMINDER:

There is a common misunderstanding that hospice does everything.

Hospice does not do everything. *Hospice can't possibly do everything.* Just as an individual caregiver can't do everything. But together, as a team, the family/caregivers and hospice can get everything done to keep you, or your loved one, home, safe and comfortable.

Your family members taking care of you, or a hired caregiver, are the primary care givers, not hospice. They are responsible for all those tasks listed above. Hospice will teach your caregivers how to do things they don't know how to do, like transferring you from your bed to a chair safely. Or changing the sheets on your bed with you in it! Hospice nurses have a lot of great tips and tricks about caring for people just like you in the same situation you're in.

CHAPTER 9

SO, WHAT HAPPENS NEXT?

I f it hasn't already been done, any equipment (DME-durable medical equipment) you need, such as oxygen, a hospital bed, walker, wheelchair, overbed table, bedside commode and a shower chair, which are the most frequently needed items, will be provided by hospice, again, at no charge.

See? Isn't hospice a wonderful program already?

Next, your team of people from hospice will start calling you to set up times for their appointments with you. They will *always have an appointment with you*, they don't just show up any time. Make sure you have a calendar handy to put all your appointments on.

It's a bit like going to the doctor, but instead of taking you to the healthcare, we bring the healthcare to you!

You may feel a bit overwhelmed at first with so many things happening so quickly. That's normal and expected. Take a break from people-ing for a while and catch your breath. This is a big deal, and I'm going to walk you through every step of the way, educate you on processes and things you've never been through before, and help you to understand what's going to be your new normal.

IMPORTANT POINTS #5

- You must assign a decision maker
- Your caregivers are responsible for your day-to-day care
- This experience can be overwhelming and emotional
- Hospice doesn't do everything

WHO ARE MY TEAM MEMBERS AND WHAT DO THEY DO?

First, is your *nurse or case manager*. The terms are used interchangeably. This nurse may be a new person to you, or the nurse may be the one who performed your admission visit. They will introduce themselves to you, set up your appointments with them, check your vital signs, look at your medications every visit and reorder your hospice medications and supplies when needed.

Your hospice nurse is your primary contact and connection to your care. Almost everything goes through this nurse.

Next is the *home health aide,* who will help with bathing, or showers, when you get to the point you can't safely do them yourself or with help from your caregiver. They only do what is assigned to them on their list provided by the nurse, which is personal care only. They don't perform housekeeping services, cooking or feeding you, just personal care for you, not anyone else in the household who may also need care. If you need housekeeping, you have to pay for that through another agency.

The *social worker* is another essential part of your team. Social workers are the gurus of community services you may be eligible for, like delivered meals or other senior benefits in your community. They're also extremely helpful if there are any issues that come up between family members. Believe me, something always comes up.

Having someone in the family on hospice brings out the best and the worst in people.

Social workers can also help you plan your end-of-life business. That means funeral and estate planning, who is going to take over your business needs, or who you want to leave your possessions to.

The *chaplain* is mandated by Medicare as an *optional* team member. The chaplains are non-denominational and are there for spiritual support, not religion. We are all spirits, no matter what, if any, religion you practice, and chaplains can be of great support to you and your family. If you do not wish to have the chaplain, you don't have to have this service. If you change your mind later, just ask your nurse or social worker to have the chaplain call you, and you can set up a visit.

The *hospice doctor, or medical director.* The medical director oversees the entire hospice operation. When you sign onto a hospice, this doctor takes over your care because your primary doctor can't fulfill the Medicare requirements. If you need medication for a new bladder infection or an old blood pressure prescription, the medical director will prescribe the needed meds for you. Just ask your nurse.

Hospice medical directors are *experts* in end-of-life care and pain control. Not every hospice patient has pain, but when patients do have pain, it's essential that their hospice nurse be able to contact a doctor 24/7 to make medication adjustments when needed. Most primary doctors or cancer specialist doctors aren't able to provide the needed 24/7 availability hospice patients require.

Having the medical director as your doctor ensures you get the fastest response possible to your needs.

After-hours, or on-call, nurse. This is a nurse you won't see very much, but if something happens at 3 AM, this is the nurse who will respond to your urgent needs. They will not be your regular nurse, but they are essential to have when urgent things come up, like a sudden change in pain level, how to administer emergency medications in the middle of the night and advising you on numerous urgent needs. They are not the nurse to call when you need supplies or have a question about your schedule. That's your regular nurse or case manager.

And lastly, another optional team member is *the volunteer*. Not all hospices have volunteers in every area they cover, but you can ask to find out. The volunteer is usually an older person. Many volunteers have been through hospice as the spouse of someone who has died, and they understand the position you and your family are in firsthand.

Volunteers go through a training program, but don't perform personal care or give medications. They will visit with you, talk with you, and read to you if you like, while giving your caregiver a bit of a break. Since the volunteers are, well, volunteering their time, we don't tell them what their schedule is or how much time they must volunteer. They tell hospice when they are available and then hospice connects them with a patient in their area.

CHAPTER 10

THE PLAN OF CARE

Every situation and every person is unique and so hospice creates a document called the Plan of Care (POC). This document and plan are adjusted according to the patient and family needs. As your condition changes, so does the POC.

Included in this document are things like:

- Your diagnosis and medications.
- The hospital equipment you need at any given time.
- How much help you need for personal care.
- Wound care or other dressings.
- Diet and food.
- Activity and sleep.

Pretty much everything that is going on with you goes on this document and is updated, when necessary, by your hospice nurse.

IMPORTANT POINTS #6:

- You will have a team of hospice people to depend on
- Hospice is provided wherever you call home
- No further outside appointments
- You call hospice instead of 911
- Your Plan of Care will change

CHAPTER 11

DON'T WAIT TOO LONG FOR HOSPICE

The trend that has unfortunately evolved over the last decade is that people are waiting until the last minute to accept hospice care.

When that happens it's a four-alarm fire for hospice to get everything into place in a hurry. That's a lot of stuff happening in your home in a very short period of time. This can be overwhelming, especially when you're ill, feel awful, or are in pain and don't know what's going to happen next.

You may have to make a choice between *quantity and quality* of your life.

Do you want to live longer if you have no quality to your life, are in constant pain and you can't do anything for yourself? If all you're doing is going to treatments, vomiting and sleeping, is that really quality of life? Only you can decide and know what quality of life is to you.

I'm encouraging you to think about what that means to you *now*, rather than waiting until later when things hit the fan. Be prepared by at least thinking about what it would take for you to want to stop treatment.

IMPORTANT POINTS #7

You have six months, and sometimes more, to have hospice care. When you choose hospice care in a crisis, hospice only has a short period of time, sometimes just a few days, (sometimes less) to work with you and your family, and that's tough on everyone. Hospice then must squeeze everything they would have had six months to help with into just a few days.

Typically, this happens with people who have a cancer diagnosis. People want to continue treatments for as long as possible, or as long as they can tolerate, which is understandable. People want their best shot with a treatment that could prolong their lives.

Unfortunately, it doesn't always turn out that way.

Chemotherapy is a poison designed to kill cancer cells, but it will also kill other cells you need to survive. Sometimes the treatment is so harsh it can contribute to a person's decline. It is unfortunate, but it does happen. I've taken care of many people who took one dose of chemo and quit immediately, due to the extreme side effects of the treatment. You will have to make a judgment as to whether it's worth it, or not, for you.

When you wait until the last minute to have hospice care, the transition from life to death can be very fast, which is upsetting to families and difficult for hospice staff, too.

Typically, people with a cancer diagnosis have a faster trajectory toward death once any life-prolonging treatments have stopped.

That is expected.

That's when you definitely need to have hospice help.

CHAPTER 12

LIFE-PROLONGING OR LIFE-SUSTAINING MEASURES

L et's talk a little about what those terms mean in real-world terms.

They are somewhat interchangeable.

Life-prolonging would generally be curative treatments, such as chemotherapy, radiation therapy or surgery to reduce or remove cancerous tissues, in the hope of a cure. These are therapies, or treatments, you would undergo after an initial cancer diagnosis and want to attempt to stop the cancer from spreading to other areas of your body. This would include blood transfusions for leukemia or other blood disorders.

Life-sustaining would be IV fluids and tube feedings.

Neither of these treatments are natural.

At end-of-life these treatments don't do what we actually want them to do. This also includes blood transfusions. Most people feel better after a blood transfusion. When they start to feel bad again, they have another transfusion and this cycle repeats until the person is no longer able to get to the clinic for transfusions, or the transfusions are no long helping. Blood transfusions are not done at home, so you would have to be able to get into the car and go to the infusion center near you, prior to signing onto hospice.

Let me reinforce that all life-prolonging and life-sustaining measures must be stopped prior to being admitted to hospice. This also includes any kind of IV hydration or nutrition.

The only exception would be if you have a tube feeding placed already, and it is your only source of nutrition because cancer has closed off your throat or esophagus. This would also need to be approved on a case-by-case basis by each hospice medical director.

Here's an example of life-sustaining measures:

If you or I were lost in the desert for a few days without water, we would require IV hydration *for survival* and to keep our organs and brains functioning properly. That is a *temporary condition* our bodies can recover from, so it is a necessary treatment for survival.

At *end-of-life* our bodies turn off the need for hydration and food. Being somewhat dehydrated is a *natural state* for the upcoming changes our bodies will go through. If we have artificially infused IV fluids at end-of-life, the fluids don't stay in the veins where we intend them to stay. Our bodies change at a cellular level during this time. Artificially administered IV fluids leak into the tissues, and into the lungs, and causes problems, like severe difficulty breathing, requiring more medications for comfort.

If you are forced to eat, or have artificial tube feedings administered, you'll vomit and be extremely uncomfortable with bloating in your stomach/intestines because the tube feeding is overloading your system that's trying to shut down. The intestinal tract slows down and often stops completely in the last days prior to death.

This is normal.

It may sound terrible, *but it's normal at end-of-life.*

. . .

How to Think About Food and Fluids on Hospice

RIGHT NOW, I give you permission to eat whatever you want as long as you can tolerate it without choking. And you can tell your family I said so!

Want a steak? *Eat it.*

Want Chinese food? *Eat it.*

Want a bag of chips? *Eat them.*

Want ice cream even though you're diabetic? *Eat it.*

Enjoy all the foods as you like. Hospice doesn't make you follow a diet. (No matter what your family says).

Hospice is about comfort care and facing the end of your life well, not on restrictions until you can't wait to die!

If you only have a few months, weeks or days to live do you want to be on a diet?

Food is a pleasure and a comfort for many of us. You should be doing things that please you right now, and that includes what have previously been considered forbidden foods.

CHAPTER 13

OTHER SIGNS THE BODY IS CHANGING

During the last transitional period prior to death our bodies try to get rid of fluid by urinating excessive amounts and/or evacuating the bowels. Turning off the appetite and the desire for any food or fluids is the first body system to change or shut down.

This happens to us all no matter what our diagnosis is. These changes are not due to disease per se, but due to the dying process. The processes and changes our bodies go through are predictable and mostly occur in a certain order. I'll walk you through those changes later in the book, going from the early stages, to transition, to imminent, and the actively dying phase.

One of the hospice doctors I worked with put it beautifully about these sorts of end-of-life treatments that patients and their families can get hung up on.

She said: *They don't prolong life. What they do is prolong the suffering.*

I've never forgotten her statement, though that conversation was over twenty years ago. Prolonging the suffering is the one thing we don't want to do.

This next information is for your family members or caregivers and it's tough stuff.

Accepting that we shouldn't feed our loved one who is ill is very difficult for a lot of families and caregivers, because we want to feed people. It's what we do as women, and as caregivers. We prepare meals, we fix favorite foods, we try to tempt our loved one to eat more, but please realize that at this time, at end of life, *food is not helpful* and will cause more difficulties than it will be helpful. Please do cook and share with others, and offer your loved one some food, but don't try to make someone eat more than they want. Sometimes just the fragrance of cooking food is enough to satisfy them. And this goes for people with and without dementia. Even those with dementia will turn away from food when they don't want it.

If someone is interested in food or fluids, they'll ask for it. Or if they've asked for something special, they may be satisfied with one or two bites of it. That's very normal. Someone who is dying has significantly lower calorie needs than you or I who are up running around expending energy.

In hospice we say *offer and encourage*, but don't try to force someone to eat or drink or make them feel bad if they don't want it. Even people with a diagnosis of dementia or Alzheimer's Disease will self-limit food and fluids, meaning they will turn away from it or push the spoon away if they are being fed. If someone isn't interested in food, they are listening to their body which is *turning off* the desire for nutrition.

Though difficult, we need to respect that change. Though you as a caregiver may not like it (and you don't have to), but at least now you can understand the why of it.

If you're able to eat and drink, items that are easy to swallow and digest are preferred. Things like yogurt, applesauce, nectar-thick liquids, puddings, tapioca, etc. They're easier to swallow and easier for the intestinal tract to digest.

More solid foods, or foods that are hard to digest, like meat, will sit for an overly long time in the gut and cause more uncomfortable problems.

Patient Story:

I was caring for a hospice patient last summer and got a distressed call from her husband, stating she was having terrible stomach pain. I asked him a series of questions about pain medication, was he giving it as instructed and what she had eaten recently.

He'd fed her a *pork chop.*

That is not easily digestible on a good day and without any having intestinal cancer. This is the time where redirecting someone to a more easily digestible food is definitely needed.

The patient required a bit more pain medication to get through the night of stomach discomfort.

CHAPTER 14

DNR-WHAT IS IT?

S ince we've just talked a bit about suffering, I'm going to talk now about a delicate topic that can lead to unnecessary suffering.

When someone is admitted to hospice, we encourage them to sign a legal DNR form which states: *Do Not Resuscitate*. Some people make this decision prior to joining hospice, but others have not, and it may be the first time someone hears about this essential topic.

Why wouldn't you want to be resuscitated? Isn't that what 911 is for? The answer to that is yes and no.

The reason for DNR status during hospice is that most of our patients are elderly and fragile, due to aging, as well as a terminal disease process and would not survive a resuscitation effort.

There is no middle ground when it comes to resuscitation. The rescue effort must go full court press, or not at all, letting nature take its course. Comfort measures are of course given.

When someone is younger, stronger, healthier and has the chance of survival from a situation like a car wreck, a heart attack or other survivable situations, it's often necessary to perform CPR to save their lives. They have a temporary situation they need to have help recovering from, such as the lost-in-the-desert scenario I described earlier.

- Temporary.
- Survivable.
- Not terminal and not an unsurvivable disease process.

Why would you want to be saved, or save someone, only for them to suffer longer and to die from the same disease process that is still present and unchanged?

Let me explain what happens during CPR (a code blue as you would hear in the hospital) and a resuscitation effort.

Due to the fragility of most of our patients they won't survive resuscitation efforts, and it is a horrifying thing to put someone through if there is no chance of long-term survival. There is a slim chance someone could survive the resuscitation effort and then be on life-support, but only for a limited time. The person would still die from their disease process.

CPR often breaks people's ribs, their sternum, and punctures lungs. It's like being in a car accident without a seatbelt, and it is brutal.

These side effects of resuscitation are painful and deadly. As our main priority in hospice is to prevent suffering, we won't deliberately inflict a treatment on someone that will lead to more suffering, as in the case of CPR.

When families are wanting to do more to sustain a person's life despite the patient suffering or lack of comfort, it's usually because the family member, or the entire family, has not accepted the inevitable death of their loved one. No matter how old they are.

That's why it's so important to have hospice care sooner rather than later, because hospice staff will have the time needed to help your family members process the changes you'll be experiencing and help them come to terms with your death.

That may sound harsh, but it's true. Many adult children are reluctant to let their parents or grandparents die even though they're suffering. Someone may be 99 years old and simply dying of old age, but the family is sometimes still reluctant to let them in peace.

Patient Story:

I received an urgent evening call from a family who said their father/husband (around 68 yrs old) had fallen out of his wheelchair and they wanted a nurse to come check him over for any injuries.

When I arrived around 8 in the evening, the patient was sitting up in his wheelchair talking with his family. I checked his vital signs (blood pressure, heart rate, breathing rate and oxygen level) and they weren't great. I asked more questions about the incident, because with falls, we nurses have to file reports.

After assessing the whole situation, I said to the patient: *I think you tried to die tonight.*

He nodded and said: *I think I did, too.*

What had happened was that he had collapsed and fallen from the wheelchair to the floor. He had had no pulse and was not rousable. The family started yelling at him and pounding on his chest for him to not die, and he started breathing again. He was able to get back into the wheelchair with help. He was totally coherent when I was talking to him during the visit and was aware of what had happened.

At the end of the visit, he said he was tired. We got him settled into his hospital bed and I left.

I received another call about 30 minutes later, that he had died. I returned to the home to verify and pronounce him deceased.

All of the stories I put into this book are true, even as bizarre as they sound. There are so many things we don't understand about the dying process, but over the years I've seen proof that we have some control over when and how we die.

CHAPTER 15
FOR FAMILIES

This is a question for family members and caregivers: When it comes to letting go of your loved one there are some tough questions you have to ask yourself:

How old does someone have to be and/or how much suffering do they have to go through before you'll let them go?

How selfish are you going to be at the time your loved one is dying? Are you willing to set aside your own needs so your loved one doesn't suffer needlessly?

This is an area I encourage you (as a family member) to look internally at your thoughts, your emotions, and your decisions. Are you making decisions that are in the best interest, and for the greatest comfort of your loved one, or are you making decisions to keep them alive, so you won't be in emotional pain?

There are going to be conflicts. One way to approach them is by asking about every issue: what is in my loved one's best interest?

*If there are family members, who I call *Bomb Droppers*,

that come in cause a lot of chaos, then leave, then they don't really have the right to any input or opinions.

Just because they are related, or close friends, doesn't mean they have the right to come in and cause problems. (These days drama is everywhere)

Only people who are calm, cooperative and helpful should be allowed near the patient and the situation. If a visitor, no matter who they are, can't comply with those guidelines, then they don't get to visit. Period. End of story.

You can post a note on the outside of the front door if you like limiting visit times and behavior.

The hospice social worker is especially helpful for mediating with family members who are in disagreement with each other. (Polite way of saying they're fighting and at each other's throats!)

But don't give up. If you are fighting for what is right for your loved one and what they have already decided they want, then you are going to be the winner. You may have little to no relationship later with the people who are causing chaos at the time.

People generally show you who they are by their behavior. If they are kind and giving, they will demonstrate this. If they are self-serving and foolish, they will demonstrate that as well. Stress, especially this kind of stress, brings out the best and the worst in people.

TAKE A BREAK

~

This is a good place to take a break and digest the information you've read so far. Maybe write down some questions that have come up. Have a cup of tea or coffee or something soothing and take a few deep breaths. This is a lot to think about.

CHAPTER 16

LET'S TALK ABOUT MEDICATIONS

Medications which are *related to comfort* or are considered *related to your diagnosis* and are *not* life-sustaining medications are covered 100%. There are no co-pays.

Example: pain medication often causes constipation, so hospice will pay for the constipation medicine because the pain medicine has caused it.

Things like oral chemotherapy drugs would *not be covered*, as they go under the category of life-prolonging or curative treatment and should be stopped prior to hospice care. If you have some pills left when you accept hospice and want to finish them that's okay, but you don't have to. They will not be renewed when you are finished with them, and there may be a specific way these meds need to be disposed of, too. Please let your nurse know when you are going over your medications if you will or will not be taking those pills.

There will be a *Comfort Kit* or *Comfort Pack* of medications ordered shortly after you are admitted to hospice. This package will be delivered to your home, or you will pick it up at the local pharmacy and is for *emergency needs*. Every hospice patient will have one in their home.

<u>What's in the kit</u>: There are a few doses of several medications for the most common symptoms you could experience at end-of-life, like nausea or vomiting, constipation, fever, anxiety or agitation, pain, excessive oral/lung secretions/phlegm or shortness-of-breath.

For the time being, you put the kit in your refrigerator and ignore it, but it needs to remain with you, not taken to the home of another family member or caregiver. Your nurse will go through it with you and your caregiver, so you, and they, will know how to administer any medications needed. The reason for having such a kit of meds in the home is extremely important.

When pain changes, or symptoms come up, they come up *fast* and often happen in the middle of the night when pharmacies are closed. (In smaller towns there are no 24-hour pharmacies) Having this kit handy with the medications you need right at your fingertips will keep you comfortable and at home. Not having essential medications like this has caused many patients and their families to call 911 because of pain or breathing trouble. It's much better to have these medications available and not need them, rather than need them and not have them.

The reason we tell everyone to put the kit in the refrigerator is if you or your family call the after-hours nurse at 3 AM and you can't remember where the kit is, the nurse will remind you to get it from the refrigerator.

A caution about two of the medications that are likely to be in the Comfort Pack, so it doesn't come as a surprise to you. Lorazepam is for anxiety or agitation and liquid Morphine Sulfate is for pain and shortness-of-breath. Both are oral medications.

Both are narcotics.

They are used by every hospice patient except for someone who has a documented allergy, and then we find a substitute that is also a narcotic.

The reason we must go to narcotics is that by this time, you've likely already been through every other medication available and are no longer getting relief with those meds, or you're already on a narcotic for pain and less potent medications wouldn't be useful in controlling your symptoms.

Please note that you are not going to become an addict. Read that line again. *You are not going to become an addict.*

You will be monitored by your nurse and the medical director while you're on these medications. They're given for a specific medical reason, *not for recreation*, like people out on the streets use them for. And you won't run out.

I do joke around when I can with my patients when I can, and this is one area where a little humor is helpful. When someone raises a concern that they'll be taking narcotics and afraid they'll become an addict, I say: *I don't see any little old ladies knocking over liquor stores to support their drug habits, do you?*

Because it doesn't happen that way! Our minds can certainly take us down a dark, scary alley in this time of the opioid crisis, but listen to your nurse who is highly trained in administering these medications and will only recommend them when the time is right.

That's a significant difference from recreational drugs. Please do not spend your time or energy worrying about this. You will be educated about these medications, their use, how and when to administer them and the first time you use any medication from the Comfort Kit, you can be on the phone with a nurse to walk you through it.

Many times, over the years, I've had patients resist taking the liquid Morphine for their breathing or pain. Only when they were desperate enough would they try it. Every patient was extremely surprised at how quickly and effectively the Morphine worked. Most of those patients said something like: I wish I'd tried this six months ago!

This liquid Morphine is super-concentrated, so you don't have to take much of it, just a few drops. It goes under the tongue, and is quickly absorbed there, nearly as fast as giving it in an IV. We can give this medication to you even if you're unconscious. That's one of the wonderful benefits of liquid Morphine.

This Morphine is short-acting, so only stays in the system for a few hours, but the relief experienced can be profound. It is not used to kill people or knock people out until they die. That's another misconception about hospice I hope to eliminate with the information provided in this book.

Keep an open mind about the medications in the Comfort Kit, as they may be the meds you need when you least expect it.

An unfortunate word of caution: if you suspect someone in your household, a visitor, or neighbor, could potentially take/steal any of your medications, you can get a lock-box to store them in. Speak with your hospice nurse about this directly. You wouldn't be the first person to have concerns about this issue. Hospice will do everything they can to keep you and your medications safe.

Medication changes.

Pharmaceutical expenses are the highest cost to hospice and when you come onto hospice *your medications will be changing*. What that means is the medical director will look at your medication list and try to pare it down to the essentials.

Things that are no longer helpful when someone is at end-of-life are medications for cholesterol, supplements of any sort, and vitamins.

Supplements can often be a choking hazard due to the large size of some of them and they should not be crushed. People often have difficulty swallowing at some point and many supplements are just too large for people to safely swallow.

Due to changes in the ability of the intestinal tract to absorb nutrients, supplements are generally no longer utilized by the body. It's a waste of money and effort to continue taking them, so consider letting go of the supplements and unnecessary medications.

Except Thyroid Medication

A different kind of supplement would be thyroid replacement medicine. Yes, it's a supplement, but this one you should continue to take until you no longer can. The thyroid hormone helps regulate many body systems, and you could feel poorly if you stop it, and it's a small tablet. Hospice doesn't cover payment for it, so you would continue to pay for it the way you normally would at your chosen pharmacy. Hospice will facilitate reordering it at your pharmacy if needed.

Hospice wants to focus on giving you the best care and comfort possible during the time you have and that includes streamlining or reducing your number of medications. Some people are on a ton of medications that require a lot of work to keep organized and people get sick of taking so many pills every day. Letting go of, or stopping some of them, will certainly lighten that load and the efforts you or your caregiver have been making to keep them all in line.

Shortly after you sign onto hospice, you'll receive a written list of medications the hospice medical director has approved of for your care. This list will change as your condition changes. If you have an increase in pain your pain medication dose or the medication itself may change.

- It goes on the list.
- If you develop a bladder infection you may be prescribed an antibiotic.
- It goes on the list.
- If you need oxygen, well, you guessed it...
- It goes on the list.

Medicare requires you have a current list of all medications you're prescribed, like the Comfort Kit, be in your home. Though you might not currently be taking the medications in the Comfort Pack, they are still in your home and are prescribed to you, so they will be on the list.

Unconventional Medications

If you are using cannabis for pain or other symptoms such as anxiety or sleep, please let your hospice team know about it. We are not there to judge you or the legality of using this substance. We only want to know about it so your other medications can be adjusted if needed. Hospice doesn't cover the cost of this drug, and the laws are ever-changing regarding the legality of it, varying state by state.

You will need to do your own research on this. Cannabis is sought more frequently than ever by people with pain and other chronic disorders, so it is coming up more frequently for people on hospice care. This issue will continually evolve, and any information placed here could be out of date in a few days.

. . .

DELIVERY **Of Your Medications**

Some hospices will have all medications sent by Fed-Ex to your doorstep, so be on the lookout for unexpected packages sitting by your door. (Bring them inside so Porch Pirates don't steal them) Fed-Ex mostly doesn't ring the doorbell or knock to let you know there is a package. Other hospices use local pharmacies that will deliver, or you can pick up your medications. Your nurse will tell you what your hospice does.

The hospice staff doesn't carry medications in their vehicles. *They are not allowed to transport medications from the pharmacy to you.* Pharmacies have safety procedures they go through for their own staff to deliver medications.

This is a huge safety issue for hospice staff. Staff used to deliver medications as a courtesy to their patients. Unfortunately, too many hospice nurses have been mugged, assaulted, or their vehicles broken into for those medications, so it's no longer done that way.

Either you will have medications delivered to your home, or someone will need to pick up your medications.

As stated before, hospice doesn't do everything. Hospice certainly will order the medications, but getting the meds to you requires some participation on your part.

Keeping Medications Organized

Get a small bin (doesn't have to be new or fancy) or plastic container and keep all of your medication bottles in it and in a handy place so your nurse can look at them quickly during visits. The nurse is required to check your medications at every visit so meds can be reordered when needed. We don't want you to run out over a weekend, or a holiday, and the best way to prevent that is checking your medications at every visit and reordering a two-week supply.

Medicare only allows a two-week supply of medications to be ordered at a time. The reason is that doses of medications change quickly, and sometimes people don't need a two-week supply. (Meaning that sometimes people die before that two-week period and don't use all of those medications.)

Staff are required to reduce waste when possible, which includes medications and supplies. We don't want to leave lots of full pill bottles in your home, and you can't stockpile supplies, either.

Leftover medications can't be returned to the pharmacy for credit, not even medications that are unused or unopened due to the possibility of medication tampering. It's unfortunate, but it's the law at this time.

Staying Organized and Keeping Track of Medications

The best suggestion I can give you is to keep a spiral notebook readily available for you and your caregivers. This is where to write notes and record when medications are given so no one forgets, and medications are given when they're supposed to be given.

This notebook is incredibly helpful for everyone to keep track of pain medications and when the last dose was given. You can't count on your memory or your caregiver's memory. Your nurse will need this information when adjusting the dose of your medications for pain or other symptoms.

It's also a great place to record bowel movements for everyone to see. (Oh, the joy!) There are no secrets in hospice.

Often, there are multiple caregivers in the home and multiple people administering medications, so this simple notebook helps everyone.

IMPORTANT POINTS #8

- Narcotics will be ordered.
- Medications will change.
- Hospice medications related to your diagnosis are covered.
- A Comfort Kit will be delivered.
- Supplies Hospice Covers.

CHAPTER 17

WHAT HOSPICE COVERS AND DOESN'T COVER

Hospice does not cover 100% of anything: diapers, bed pads (chux), or wipes for cleaning up bowel movements. Hospice provides *supplemental amounts* of briefs and wipes which are the two biggest items families are wanting to have for free. These are expensive items for families to buy out of pocket all the time, so hospice does help with that, but they do not provide 100% of these items.

An easy way to remember what hospice covers and doesn't cover is: if it's related to the patient's diagnosis, or comfort, it's covered. That applies to medications, equipment and supplies. If you want a particular brand of something hospice doesn't carry, you'll have to purchase that item yourself. Hospices have specific medical supply warehouses they order from. If you're particular about a certain item(s), you'll have to purchase those specific brands yourself.

If you have wounds, such as a bedsore with a dressing on it, hospice will provide the needed supplies for this. The supplies will generally be different than the exact one(s) used by the hospital you were in.

Your hospice nurse doesn't change the dressing every day. Most wounds only need to have the dressing changed 1-2 times weekly or if soiled. The nurse will teach your caregiver/family member how to change the dressing if it needs to be done in between nursing visits. This can be scary for some people, but your caregiver will be trained in how to do these needed procedures.

This also includes any tubes in your body that require care, such as a urinary catheter, that needs to be emptied 1-2 times per day. The nurse will teach you and/or your caregiver how to do this.

Nurse Trick: when someone is bedbound a helpful thing to do is to buy some large or XL T-shirts (they must be a little large) Cut the shirts up the back, but don't cut the neckband of the shirt. This way you can pop it over your loved one's head, put their arms in the sleeves and viola! You have a patient gown that's easy to get on and off.

Hospice patients are coming out of hospitals sicker and with more tubes than ever, so your family will need to care for certain tubes or drains in between nurse visits. The supplies will be provided by hospice, but the care must be provided by you or your family.

CHAPTER 18

WHAT DO YOU DO NEXT?

N ow, you do your thing. Live your life. Be happy and comfortable for as long as you can.

Remember a while ago when I talked to you about not wasting time? Well, that starts *now*. Once you're adjusted to having people in your home and you have your schedule made for your visits, it's time to live your life.

On hospice you *do not have to be homebound.* (Meaning that leaving your home requires a significant effort on your part and the assistance of another person, plus you can only go out on a limited basis to needed things, like doctor visits, pharmacy, church, and minimal things) If you're on home healthcare, you do have to be homebound.

Different rules for hospice, though. You can go out as you like, go to the movies, dinner, visit family, go fly fishing in another state and anything else you can think of that you want to, and can, do.

Just keep up the communication with hospice so your team doesn't come to your home when you're not there. Be respectful of their time and energy as they are respectful of yours.

COMMUNICATION

COMMUNICATION WILL MAKE OR BREAK ANY RELATIONSHIP AND THAT INCLUDES THE ONE YOU HAVE WITH YOUR HOSPICE TEAM. COMMUNICATION GOES IN ALL DIRECTIONS: FROM HOSPICE TO YOU, YOU TO HOSPICE, AMONG HOSPICE TEAM MEMBERS AND IN BETWEEN YOU AND YOUR FAMILY OR CAREGIVERS. ALL DIRECTIONS. NO JUDGEMENTS. JUST COMMUNICATION.

Don't understand something you know you've been told about ten times already? Ask again.

- Afraid of something? Ask your nurse to explain it to you in a way you understand. (When you understand something, it usually reduces the fear).
- Want to tell your spouse or partner something, but are hesitating because of how they might react? Tell them anyway.
- You may not have time to clear the air later.

CHAPTER 19
NURSE VISIT

L et's go through what a typical nurse visit will look like.

Your nurse arrives at the appointed time, or 30 minutes before or after, but in the ballpark of the set time. There are no exact times in hospice. The nurse's previous visit could have run longer, or ended more quickly, than expected. Or there could have been a traffic issue that delayed your nurse's visit. The nurse can't control those things, so cut 'em a break. It's not disrespectful if your nurse is a few minutes early or late. You'd want your nurse to stay as long as necessary with you, right? So, your nurse will stay as long as necessary with her other patients as well. (I'm sure you've had to wait in your doctor's office because they were running late, right?)

Be ready a few minutes earlier than the appointed time, then relax until your nurse arrives. Be respectful of their time, as they are of yours.

Nurses also have meetings that aren't scheduled around their patients and that is unfortunate, but that's the way the business world works. Meetings are scheduled, and we attend them whether we like it or not. (Mostly we don't like it!)

You'll get to know your nurse, and they'll get to know you. They'll be able to schedule your visits as needed during the work week, which is Monday through Friday, from approximately 8 AM to 5 PM. Then the after-hours, night or weekend nurses will take over for emergencies.

The first few visits may be longer or shorter than you thought, and it varies depending on what's going on with you. If you're comfortable, have all your meds, no issues, then the visit can be as short as fifteen minutes. If something else is going on, the nurse will adjust her visit time to accommodate and make sure you're comfortable before leaving.

The nurse will check your vital signs, just like at the doctor's office, and do an assessment. This means listening to your heart and lungs, look for swelling around your ankles and lower legs. Your skin will be checked for any bruising, or skin breakdown, which could lead to a pressure sore or a skin ulceration that could lead to an infection.

Your nurse is the eyes and ears of the medical director and reports directly to that person about your condition. If something comes up, like a suspected bladder infection, your nurse will report this to the medical director and get the necessary medications ordered for you.

The nurse will also get nosy about your bowels and bladder *every single visit*. At first it may be embarrassing, but you'll get used to it, and it's necessary information for your nurse to know.

It's very important to keep track of your bowel movements in your spiral notebook. That may sound like too much information you don't want to deal with, but I assure you it's necessary. Pain medications often cause constipation, and constipation can lead to a life-threatening bowel blockage which you do not want. Most people at end-of-life would not survive surgery for a bowel blockage, so hospice works very hard to prevent this by managing your bowel status. (Sounds like great fun, doesn't it?)

I know, that is just the least interesting topic you could think of to discuss with a stranger in your home, but it's necessary.

CHAPTER 20

PATIENT STORY: BODILY FUNCTIONS

One weekend I was on-call and received a visit request from a patient's daughter about his severe constipation. He had dementia and the daughter wasn't certain he was giving her accurate information about his bowel status, but she thought he hadn't had a BM in several days. I made a visit, assessed the patient and sure enough, he was impacted. (Impacted is when the rectum is full of stool that the person can't pass without assistance.)

So, we all had the unfortunate experience of me disimpacting him. I won't go into the gory details here, but it was not pleasant for him to have me pull stool out of his rectum manually. His bowel movement was then fixed, but it was a painful experience for him. (It was a definite pain in the backside!)

I updated the daughter on the results and said goodbye to her. As I was heading down the hall toward the door, I heard him exclaim to his daughter: *That woman just saved my life!*

Sometimes it can feel like that, but it's much easier to keep track of your bowel movements in the notebook.

URINATION IS ALSO IMPORTANT. As people change and decline, their interest in food and fluids is reduced, and this will reduce the amount of urine you make in a day. That gives the nurse information about the health status of your kidneys, whether they are working well or not. The color of urine will also change to being darker and a little stinky. That doesn't automatically mean you have a bladder infection. If you can increase your water (yes, water-most people do not like drinking plain water, but it really helps all body systems work better) intake this helps a lot. This change and reduction in urination is normal and expected.

We want you to be aware of, and understand, what is normal, rather than be fearful when there is a change.

A change is a change. Doesn't mean it's automatically bad. It's a sign that your body systems are changing. This information will help your nurse guide you and your family through more upcoming changes.

If all you want to drink is coffee, tea or soft drinks, try to drink a glass of water for each one of those drinks, as they all contribute to dehydration. Anything containing caffeine is a mild diuretic.

OTHER AREAS your nurse will ask you about, not in any particular order, but include:

- Medications
- Eating

- Drinking
- Choking with food/fluids
- Appetite
- Breathing
- Cough
- How you're sleeping, or not sleeping
- Your skin
- Falls
- Pain
- How your family or caregiver is coping with everything

Your nurse may do some charting, or documenting notes of your visit, on a small computer or other electronic device while in your home. This has become increasingly normal as hospice programs have gone away from paper charting. Just as your doctor has charted on the computer during visits with you at the office, the same is true of hospice staff.

Nurse visits will be the most frequent kind of visits you will have.

Will The Medical Director Visit?

Medical director visits have changed since the pandemic, so check with your hospice at admission to find out what they do. Prior to the pandemic every hospice patient had an in-person visit at their home by the medical director. This was wonderful for the patients and families to meet the doctor who would be managing their care, and for the doctor to lay eyes directly on their new patient.

Some hospices have gone to video visits. Your nurse will use their phone, so you don't have to know how to do this.

The nurse will arrive and get the doctor on a video call on their phone, and you can talk directly to, and see, the medical director, and they can see you. This is less than ideal, but it's getting the job done. I don't know if in-person visits for the medical directors will return to what they were pre-pandemic, so check with your hospice.

CHAPTER 21
WEIRD STUFF

H ospice, death and dying are heavy topics, so I try to lighten the mood when I can. I tell patients and their families that *anything weird is normal in hospice.* Not to make light of a serious situation, but you must understand that the things you're going to experience that *seem* pretty crazy are *very normal and expected at end of life,* but they are very different from your usual behavior and activity.

You may have a personality change and become withdrawn. That's expected, too. You may decide you need to clean your entire house top to bottom before you can die. You may want to give away all your possessions. Any number of things can come up or suddenly feel like an emergency to get done before you can die.

Those are all normal. Everyone does their thing differently, so your death and the way you approach it will also be unique.

This book is designed to help you understand that the weirdness is normal, expected and can give your family some very interesting memories to look back on later. Not all deaths are scary. Not all deaths are pleasant. Most fall somewhere in between, and that's what we're going to discuss next.

THE DYING PROCESS

Now, I'd like to tell you about what happens as you get closer to your dying time. This is a very individual, and very unique process, but every body changes in similar ways. What I'll explain next are changes most people experience at some time during this process.

There's an old saying that people die as they live. This means that if someone has a more easy-going personality, they will probably have an easier time letting go and passing on. Those who are more uptight personalities, or controllers, have a harder time letting go. ((Those kinds of personalities typically will often have heart disease and/or lung disease).

CHAPTER 22
PHASES OF DYING:

Normal Life-you're doing your thing normally. Eating, drinking, sleeping, engaging in activities or hobbies, and family events.

Decline-you're less engaged in life, less interested in activities, food or fluids. Just winding down, sleeping more. This phase can last for days or weeks to months.

Transitional Phase-this phase can last from a few days to a few weeks. At this time, you can do what I call *walking in both worlds*. This means that you're being appropriate in answering your nurse or caregiver or engaged in an activity. Other times you can have *visions*. You may see dead loved ones, hear music, see angels, children or other people you don't recognize, but somehow do, yet they are not visible to others around you. (These are not hallucinations).

You may have a conversation with your Uncle Joe who's been dead for many years and still be able to tell your caregiver what you want for lunch.

One patient of mine saw a beautiful meadow with tress, birds and fluffy clouds. Another person saw angels on every surface in his room: the bed, the dresser, chairs, and he loved it.

Exactly what you see, or experience, will be different from anyone else's experience, because we're all different souls.

<u>Fear at time of death:</u> in all of the 27 years I've been a hospice nurse I've never seen anyone be frightened at the time of death. Never. In weeks prior, when there are unresolved issues, there can be anxiety and some fear, but once those issues are resolved there is no fear.

There is usually peace and a sense of calm for the patient. Or they are sleeping nearly 24/7.

<u>Pre-Terminal Anxiety</u>

This is a special kind of anxiety generally occurring between 24-48 hours prior to when someone dies.

This is usually a result of something unresolved:

- leaving loved ones
- not seeing someone who is important to you before you go
- needing reassurance that your mate or spouse will be taken care of when you go
- that your business will be taken care of
- or a million other things

The issue can also be about something your family isn't aware of. You may not be able to verbalize what the issue is, either, but it's bugging you enough to make you restless and anxious. This happens to both younger and older patients.

What family can do at this time is to reassure the patient that everything will be fine, their kids or spouse will be taken care of by other family members, that the business will be handled or beloved pets will be cared for.

Patient Story:

Another hospice nurse told me a story about one of her patients who was lingering for days, and it appeared that everything possible was taken care of. The man had never married, had no children, and all end-of-life business was wrapped up.

Something clicked with my friend, and she leaned over and spoke close to his ear. She said: I will take care of your cat.

The man died 15 minutes later. That was what he needed to know, and he could let go knowing his cat would be looked after by someone he knew.

FAMILIES: You may figure out what your loved one needs to hear, but you may not, because the issue is deeply personal to your loved one. That's okay. It happens. Keep doing what you're doing, and this agitation phase will subside.

Symptoms of Pre-Terminal Anxiety Include:

RESTLESSNESS: you want up in your chair, you want back to bed, you want to go for a walk, you want to lie down. No place seems very comfortable to you for very long. You may pace or continually try to get out of bed if you are weak and lack the strength to get up.

Anger: sometimes anger comes out, but you don't know

why you're upset. You may snap at your caregiver or family, and are generally out of sorts, but can't put a finger on why.

If your loved one is unconscious and this happens, you may see them be agitated, restless in the bed, and fidgety for no apparent reason. This is still pre-terminal anxiety.

Sleeplessness: you may be exhausted, but your brain will not allow you to rest because of the weight of an issue that's on your mind, and in your spirit, that must be dealt with. You may be awake for many hours at a stretch and sleep only for brief amounts over a few days.

Loss of appetite: nothing sounds or smells good. For a minute you think you want something, then when it's brought to you it doesn't taste good, or you're satisfied with just a few bites of it.

Some, or all, of these behaviors are necessary for the spirit to work on the issue going on internally.

Anti-anxiety medications may be needed *at much higher doses* during this period to keep you safe, from crawling out of bed, and falling on the floor.

Please note: it may seem to your family or caregiver that a phenomenal amount of medication is being given to you during this period, but it isn't working. That's because what you're wrestling with is a spiritual issue, and we can't medicate the spirit, only the body it's housed in.

For some people the pre-terminal anxiety is a necessary process to go through due to the deeply personal issue they're dealing with.

What happens after pre-terminal anxiety resolves?

Once the issue is dealt with internally, then the restlessness stops. You'll sleep better, might be more interested in eating again and seem to be back to your usual self, but that only lasts for a short time.

CHAPTER 23

THE LAST SUPPER

After the pre-terminal anxiety phase resolves, you/your loved one may have little to no memory of the events of the previous days.

You may come out of it very hungry because you haven't eaten for a few days and your caregivers are exhausted from their sleepless nights spent keeping you safe.

Your mental capacity can suddenly become very sharp, and you feel bright, energetic and better than ever! You call the family over to have a meal together. You might want foods you haven't had in a long time, like steak, or roasted chicken, pumpkin pie or whatever you love.

Your family will come over and have the best time they've had with you in months! You're engaged, your memory is clear, and you have no trouble feeding yourself. It's just like old times, and you feel amazing. Your family is happy to see the old you shine through again.

At the end of this meal, you'll likely be very tired because you've expended a considerable amount of energy for a few days being agitated, so it's no wonder you're tired.

The next morning your family is thrilled that you've had such a wonderful improvement in your condition, but when they go to wake you, they can't. You're in a coma.

Or you've already died in your sleep.

That's why I call that last surge of energy *The Last Supper*. It's really a goodbye from you to your family. You may not say it like that, but when looking back on that time, your family will be able to view it that way. Some things are easier to look back on later than to figure out in the moment, and this is one of those times.

This last meal was a last gift from you to them, for them to have a glimpse again of how you used to be, it is a memory for them to cherish after you're gone.

The abrupt change from the previous day to how you are afterward can be quite a shock for your family. Deep inside, a little voice had tried to convince them you were getting better and now that little voice is telling them it isn't true. They have to face reality all over again, and it's sad for them to have their hopes dashed.

If this is the case, your family should call hospice to update your nurse on the change in condition or death. This change can be devastating to your family, and they will need extra emotional and grief support from hospice.

Not everyone has a Last Supper moment. Some people move from the transitional phase to the actively dying phase described next.

Actively Dying-This is then next step after the transitional phase. You'll sleep more, possibly 24/7, and very difficult to rouse, if you're rousable at all. Your ability to look outside yourself is gone.

Families: this is a time where you might see your loved one look at you when you call their name or touch them, but they appear to be *looking through you*. That's a significant sign they are having a conversation with the other side. They aren't seeing you and can no longer interact with you.

At this point I ask families to take a hands-off approach as much as possible, to not try to engage their loved on in conversation or try to wake them up to eat, drink or take medications because it will pull them out of this essential phase and only prolong the dying process.

Many people become unarousable at this point no matter what stimuli (touch or voice) is used. They're simply too deep in their processing to be brought out of it.

That's okay. *That's what is supposed to happen, and it's normal.* Your loved one is well into their journey to the other side. This is a significant part of the dying process.

Your loved one will still be able to hear and understand what people are saying, but they won't be able to respond because their focus is deeply inward.

This, again, is necessary. It's necessary for them to emotionally pull back from their family so they can go deep inside to do their inner work. This inner work must be done for someone to pass and have what we consider a good death.

This can be a hard time for families, as your loved one withdraws from you more and more. This change makes it real that they will soon be gone.

There are breathing changes they may experience, and you can see, as most people do. This includes a repeated pattern of breathing (of course, two doctors named it after themselves) that happens because the brain is changing and losing its ability to function normally. This will continue to progress and is unlikely to return to a normal breathing pattern.

They may develop a fever, but it's also due to brain

changes that it isn't able to heat/cool normally, not from an infection. We still treat the fever with Tylenol (suppositories, though) for comfort.

They won't be able to take any pills or other medications except for the ones in the Comfort Pack. Hospice will have the family stop giving anything else except for those comfort medications.

Remember: most medications in the Comfort Pack are absorbed in the mouth, so they don't have to be swallowed. Even if the liquid dribbles out, they will have absorbed the medication in the liquid almost instantly.

Imminently Dying: This is the last phase, and family will see changes that can be harder for them to watch than for their loved one to experience. The breathing changes continue, and they may experience increased mouth and lung secretions, or phlegm, because they're not being swallowed as usual. There is a medication in the comfort pack for this which can be a pill that can be crushed and applied to the inner cheek, or a liquid medication, both absorbed in the mouth. This helps control the secretions but doesn't eliminate them entirely. Turning your loved one side-to-side periodically, will help shift the fluid around so it's not as noisy.

This phase can go on for a few hours or a few days.

CHAPTER 24

PATIENT STORY:

A patient I admitted at noon, then died at 4 pm. We didn't even have time to get a hospital bed to the home before he died. He was an ex-Air Force/commercial airline pilot, in his late 60's. He had a very controlling personality, and he was never going to agree to hospice, per his wife. As soon as he couldn't say no, his wife said yes, and brought us in. I could see at the time I was admitting him that he was actively dying, so I had to give the wife and son the fast-track hospice talk, because he wasn't going to live much longer. I knew he would be gone in a matter of hours.

I returned at 4 pm to pronounce him deceased after the family called me. When I arrived, the wife said: *he did everything you said he was going to do. He was very focused on something on the ceiling over the bed. He watched it go across the ceiling and out the window, and then he took his last breath.*

Though he resisted hospice care, it was a peaceful passing for him, and you may see your loved one have a similar experience. This gentleman was in his own bed with his family around him. They were reassured that the spirits came for him and took him with them peacefully and nothing was left unresolved. Though brief, having the patient admitted to hospice also meant that the family had access to grief support after his death.

CHAPTER 25

TAKING DEATH FOR A TEST DRIVE

After so many years of seeing this particular change in people, that's the only conclusion I've come to that makes sense. Let me explain what I mean by a *test drive*.

Sometimes people will appear that they are dying and are in the actively dying phase, remaining there for several days. They're not arousable, no matter what. Breathing changes are noticed, they don't eat, or drink, their urine output drops, and they become incontinent (unable to hold their bladder or bowels) so it really appears they're headed to their dying time.

The surprise is that after a few days of this condition, the person will then wake up and be right where they were before the incident occurred. They have no memory of being gone. No memory of the other side. No visions of a white light calling them. They simply pick up right where they left off and are usually pretty hungry and thirsty.

When they return, or recover from this incident, days or weeks can pass before they go into their true decline toward death.

CHAPTER 26
PATIENT STORY: URGENT ADMISSION

I was called urgently to a home to admit an elderly woman (in her late 80's or early 90's) who had been comatose for three days. Her family was very concerned that she was dying and wanted hospice ASAP. Given that description, I was pretty sure she was, too.

When I arrived at the home around 5 pm, I greeted the family *and the patient* who was then sitting up at the kitchen table drinking coffee, totally coherent, wondering what the fuss was all about!

As I said before, everything weird is perfectly normal in hospice. I wasn't kidding! I did admit this lady to hospice service, and she died a few weeks later.

CHAPTER 27
WHEN THE BODY STOPS RESPONDING TO TREATMENT

Another treatment people are often very attached to is blood transfusions for certain diagnoses, such as Leukemia, Lymphoma or Myeloma. Blood transfusions will refill the depleted number of blood cells circulating in the system and the patient will often feel much better within a few hours of having a blood transfusion. Unfortunately, this doesn't last very long and gets less effective over time, requiring more frequent transfusions.

As disease progresses is it's harder to get in the car and go to the infusion center. Blood transfusions can't be done in the home, so you must be able to go to the infusion clinic for them.

For many people, the deciding factor about accepting hospice, versus not accepting hospice, is when it gets too difficult for them to go to treatments. That's a good time to transition from curative, or life prolonging treatments (including blood transfusions) to comfort care only. Many times, it's a relief for both the patient and family not to make that exhausting trek to the infusion center any longer.

Each person and family must make their own decision on this.

Your doctor can make recommendations as to when to stop, or they can tell you that *they are going to stop treating* you because there is, unfortunately, no benefit in continuing further. That may sound harsh, but at some point, the body is no longer able to respond to any treatment, no matter what is thrown at it. This happens to all of us.

There are many cases of very wealthy people or celebrities who die after cancer treatments, or many kinds of life-saving treatment, so it's not about status or wealth.

If anyone in the world could have been saved by position, wealth and power it would have been Princess Diana, yet she could not be saved from her injuries in the car crash that killed her.

The issue here is not about money or affluence. It's about the body, what it can handle, what it can't, and when is the best time to say enough is enough.

It would be best for your mental and emotional health to choose to stop treatments rather than having the doctor tell you treatments are being stopped.

A lot of people at this point will feel like they're being given up on and in some respects it's true. What is really being given up on is wasting your precious time on therapy, treatment of the disease, *not the person,* that is no longer responding to treatment.

Stop for a moment and read that again, let it sit in your mind for a few minutes. *We're not giving up on you.* We're changing tactics and focusing on different goals that promote quality of life, not quantity. The disease isn't budging, so we have to change our plan.

There comes a time in everyone's life when their body will not respond to any treatment, no matter what kind. We never know when that will happen until it actually happens. The body is unable to be stimulated any longer into improvement, and that includes things like blood transfusions, IV antibiotics, oxygen or even higher level of artificial means, which means being put on life support. The body will cease functioning anyway. It is worn out.

These are hard topics to think about, to process, and to talk about, but it's essential that you do so at the earliest time you're able to. Making decisions in a crisis is the worst time to do it. Once your decisions are made, you don't have to worry about anything catastrophic happening, because you've already handled it ahead of time. You and your family will know what to do when that time comes. If nothing catastrophic happens, you're still ahead of the game.

When you make your decisions ahead of time, you give your family a priceless gift of not having to make these hard decisions for you. Their job then will be to see that your wishes are carried out.

CHAPTER 28

PERSONAL STORY: MY BROTHER

My brother died at age 55, in the summer of 2023. He had a catastrophic stroke in the brain stem at the base of the brain, which handles all basic functions like breathing and swallowing. The very basic things needed to run our human body. He was taken by Life Flight from our little town to Pittsburgh, but after a few weeks in the Neuro ICU and receiving the best of care, it became clear he wasn't going to recover any function or have any sort of normal life off of machines.

We could have left him connected to an artificial respirator with artificial tube feedings and put him in a nursing home for the rest of his life, because he couldn't breathe or eat on his own. Our family knew he would not have wanted to exist that way, because for him, that was not living. If he couldn't pursue his hobbies of hunting, fishing, target practice and driving his truck, it would not have been a life for him.

About one month before the stroke he had a conversation with our mother that he didn't think he was going to live much longer. He didn't know why and wouldn't discuss it further, but he had a sense of how much time he had left to live. This happens to a lot of people.

Though he hadn't signed any forms for DNR, our mother knew from that one conversation that he wouldn't want to be kept alive by artificial means.

Our choice, as a family, was to remove the artificial life support and let him go. He died within two hours. That told me that there was nothing left of the spirit of him, that it took just two hours for his bodily reflexes to stop.

Talking about, and processing, this kind of information related to your particular diagnosis is essential for your future processing as you prepare for the end of your life.

TAKE A BREAK

~

This is a good place to take a break, digest the information and think about how it can be applied to your life or the life of a family member.

If you're already the medical power of attorney for someone, this is excellent information for you to discuss with your loved one and your family.

Let them know you are not making the decisions but ensuring that your loved one's wishes are being carried out when they are no longer able to do so.

CHAPTER 29
SHIFT CARE

Does hospice provide shift care?

A common misconception is that hospice provides 24 -hour nursing care to every patient. That's an impossible task. There aren't enough qualified nurses in the entire country to do that.

As always, there are exceptions to rules. There are times when a person is near death *and having out of control pain*, that a hospice can provide *some* shift care on a *limited basis*. Your nurse, or other nurses, will be at your bedside to administer pain medications in higher doses and more frequently, as directed by the medical director, to get the pain under control as quickly as possible.

Read that previous paragraph again.

The shift care is *temporary and for a very specific reason*. Not everyone will have out-of-control pain at the end and some people have no pain at all, which is a wonderful thing.

When the pain is under control, the shift care ends. The family, or caregiver, once again takes over as before. This type of care is called Continuous Care, but again for a limited time. Each hospice must be able to provide this service in some fashion to comply with Medicare regulations. Speak to your hospice about how they manage this.

Some insurances may provide limited shift care. Each each policy is different, so you'll have to look at yours to see if they provide any shift care.

CHAPTER 30

WHAT HAPPENS AFTER YOU DIE?

When someone stops breathing or their heart stops due to natural disease process and they are on hospice, 911 is not notified. Hospice is notified, 24/7. As family, we want to call someone, to do something! We've been trained for decades that when there's an emergency you call 911. But not in this situation. Not at end of life.

This is an expected death, and the patient is under the care of a hospice physician, so there is no need for emergency services. If the hospice nurse finds anything suspicious at the time of the pronouncement, then they will contact the coroner or medical investigator.

This provides the dignity of death at home as promised by hospice.

- No sirens
- No firetrucks
- No ambulance
- No police officers

No one racing to a home to try to save someone who has died from natural causes.

Having emergency services respond to an expected death is a huge diversion of their time, energy and resources that are better spent in your community in other ways. Right? Can you understand and accept that? Can your family?

All hospice nurses are certified to pronounce (that's the term for it) patients who die in the home as long as they've been under the care of a physician, on hospice, and there are no suspicious circumstances. All hospice nurses are Deputy Medical Investigators and are certified by the state they work in to perform a scene investigation to make sure nothing unusual has happened and your death was natural. If the nurse determines something is suspicious in the home surrounding your death, they'll notify the Office of the Medical Investigator, Coroner, or call 911, depending on the laws in each state or county. Your hospice nurse will let you know how this will be handled.

The nurse will also handle the disposal of remaining medications, the family does not touch them, as the nurse needs to count all narcotics in the home first.

It's very important that family not try to over help by disposing of medications prior to the nurse arriving. There are processes the nurse needs to follow for their reports to Medicare and counting all medications is part of it.

In the days leading up to your passing your family will be alerted by your nurse that you're getting closer to your dying time at each visit. As you progress through the dying phases your nurse will explain each phase to your family so they will understand what to expect, what is normal and reinforcing them to call hospice, not 911.

Sometimes, a family member will panic and call 911

anyway. If that happens, please call hospice immediately afterward. The police will then have to release the scene (their term) to the hospice nurse before they can leave.

Once it's been determined that you've died, your nurse will assist your family in calling the mortuary that you (hopefully) had chosen ahead of time. If one hadn't been chosen, then your family will need to make that choice as soon as possible and let your hospice nurse know who to call. The nurse gives the mortuary the information needed for them to fill out the death certificate that the medical director will then sign.

An Exception:

If you are Native American and die on reservation or pueblo land the process is different. The governor of the pueblo or reservation may be the one who does the pronouncement and who provides the death certificates. Reservations and pueblos are considered separate, sovereign nations in this regard. Native Americans often have specific religious and cultural practices that are different from other areas. In this case, you or your family will have to let your hospice nurse know what your plans are, how you will be buried, and any support that hospice can provide.

CHAPTER 31

THE DEATH CERTIFICATE

Your family will need multiple copies of your death certificate to prove to various agencies that you have died.

Medicare, Medicaid and insurance companies will each want their own certified copy, and your family has a certain amount of time to get this information to them. Ordering more certificates at the time of your death is significantly easier and cheaper than trying to get them from the state later.

Your social worker at hospice can help your family navigate these notifications if needed.

Most mortuaries have a list of things your family will need to provide and will walk your family through their processes.

A good question for your family to ask the mortuary is: how long will it take to get the death certificates to them?

In some states when someone is cremated, the Office of the Medical Investigator must sign off on the death certificate as well as the medical director and that can add additional time to when the death certificate is available. After that process is complete, the certificate will be made available for your family.

CHAPTER 32
GRIEF OVERVIEW

Grief Support With Hospice

The stages of grief were studied and organized by Swiss psychiatrist Dr. Elizabeth Kübler-Ross in 1969. There are many resources on the internet about grief. An extensive education about grief is outside the scope of this book, but here is a brief bit of information.

This book isn't dedicated solely to grief, but this section is provided to give you an introduction to it. Grief is a book all by itself.

Grief can come with a devastating event, such as the loss of a loved one, that we'll be discussing here. Grief can also be experienced in more subtle, everyday terms, too.

Have you ever felt down or depressed if you didn't get the job you were really hoping for? Or at the loss of a pet? Or even the loss of something else important to you, like the loss of a friendship or relationship. Or even a broken memento you've treasured for years can trigger feelings of loss.

We experience grief in little doses almost every day.

How you cope with the little griefs can help you cope with the bigger griefs after someone you love has died. As you think about this, you'll see that you've experienced grief that wasn't recognized as grief in many aspects of your life.

Remember: you may not get over the loss of a loved one or many other griefs, but you do *get through them* with help, support and time. None of this is easy.

CHAPTER 33
HOSPICE GRIEF SUPPORT

Through hospice, a patient's family and caregivers have access to grief support, often called *bereavement*, for up to 13 months. It's not individual therapy. If your family members need therapy, they should pursue that individually through their own healthcare system.

Hospice has a well-organized grief support team to assist families in many phases of their grief, from anticipatory grief before their loved one dies, and afterwards.

This is generally done in a small group, and the times vary for each hospice. Your family will be contacted by the bereavement coordinator within a few days of the death of their loved one to check in on them and get them set up for grief support if needed.

Not everyone needs grief support. Often people have their own support systems already in place, and you can look for grief support in the following ways:

- Other family members
- Their church

- Friends
- Books
- Gardening
- Being in nature
- Pets make very good listeners, but they aren't the only answer if you need more help

Processing grief takes time, patience, going through the phases as they come up and continuing to live your life. Sometimes getting involved in something, like a class or group, to help distract a person from the immediacy of the grief is helpful, but the old cliché is true: *it takes time*.

My recommendation is that if someone feels stuck in their grief, then that's a good time to seek organized grief support.

CHAPTER 34

THE PHASES OF GRIEF

- Denial
- Anger
- Bargaining
- Depression
- Acceptance

The list above is the general order in which people experience grief. This applies to the person who is facing the end of their life as well as people who will miss them after they die. Some people will go back and forth in the phases. Some people will die in anger and never get to acceptance. Some family members will also stay angry and bitter for longer periods rather than letting themselves experience the pain of loss.

Let's have a look at these phases more closely. The descriptions are addressed to the patient, but they apply to family members, friends and caregivers as well. Children also experience loss and have different needs outside the scope of this book. Please seek someone skilled in children and grief.

Denial

Denial is a time at the beginning of your illness when you're not accepting it. No, you think, I can't have X disease or cancer. I just can't! I don't have time for this. I have children to raise. Or my granddaughter is getting married in four months, and I have to be there. Or any number of other phrases you can think of that try to push away the thought of something that is going to bring about the end of your life.

If you ever hear yourself saying: no, no, no, no, no, that's denial, no matter what situation you're in, from a relationship breakup, to loss of a job, or the death of a pet.

Denial is a very powerful coping mechanism we all have inside of us. It protects our minds and our emotions from difficult situations, or truths, that can be very painful to think about and experience.

Denial prolonged can interfere with the acceptance of the truth as well. Often, the person with the disease has an easier time accepting it than the family does.

Anger

Anger is very understandable. You may be angry at your doctor or the medical establishment in general for not catching your illness sooner or not having a treatment to cure your illness. There are many things to be angry about, including God or your higher power, for not fixing it.

Your family may be angry at you for not going to your doctor sooner and that's hard for many people to express. Instead, they take their anger out on the doctor for not having the magical ability to diagnose an illness on the spot.

It's easier to be angry at a person or the medical establishment than at a disease, because the disease doesn't care. It just keeps on going, tearing its way through your body.

Bargaining

You may have heard the phrase: there are no atheists in fox holes. That's an excellent example of bargaining. Soldiers under horrendous, life-threatening, conditions will often bargain with their God that if they survive the situation they're in, they'll become a priest, or work in the family business, or whatever it is they'll do to get out of the situation alive. If I get this, I'll do that. That's bargaining.

You may think, if I live through surgery or chemo, I'll be a better person, appreciate life more and stop being so _____. You fill in the blank. That's bargaining.

Depression

This is a pivotal phase in the grief process. This applies to you, the patient, but to your family and friends as well. Each of you will have a different process of grief, sometimes starting well before your death.

You are where you are in the grief process and trying to hurry it up doesn't work. It takes time to process everything.

Acceptance

This is the final phase of the grief process. Once you get to acceptance, you've gone through all the phases of grief, but maybe not in the order listed. You may have spent some time bouncing back and forth between bargaining and anger. That's also normal.

A few more aspects of grief that can happen are:

Anticipatory grief. This occurs as you progress through your illness and your family watches you decline before their eyes. They know that the big grief is coming up and to help reduce the pain they know is coming, they start grieving your loss before you die. They're anticipating what's coming up and trying to get ahead of it.

Everyone goes through the phases differently and there's no set time frame to remain in any one phase.

Just as your life has been unique and individual, so will be your dying process. Just go with it. Be where you are in the process. Don't try to force yourself to be happy on days where you clearly aren't.

Delayed grief. This sometimes occurs for your family or caregiver when there simply isn't time to grieve at the time of your death.

Some Reasons Grief Can Be Delayed:

Taking care of someone else needing attention
Caring for small children
Caring for another elderly person
Going back to work right away
Having to move right away

Something that takes up the majority of someone's time and mental energy interferes in the grief process. Some family members have told me they hadn't grieved properly the death of someone who had died many years ago due to life circumstances. That's how delayed grief can be for some people, yet they have continued to go on with their lives.

Delayed grief can be an issue if delayed for too long. Sometimes when a parent with multiple children loses a child, they can't grieve that loss due to the needs of the other children.

People will say how well this person is coping, when in fact, they aren't coping at all, they've only delayed the inevitable. It will hit them at some time in the future and we can never predict when that will be. It could be when they're driving down a long stretch of highway and it hits. It could be when they have interrupted sleep for several nights in a row. It could be anything that can be a trigger, or it can be subtle and sneak up on them when they least expect it.

New griefs, a new loss of some sort, often bring up old griefs and then the person is hit with more than one grief experience at the same time. That's when grief can become complicated, and they should seek professional help.

TAKE A BREAK

~

This is another good place to take a break, digest what you've read and figure how it applies to your situation.

Everyone will go through a grieving process, and everyone will do it differently. That doesn't make anyone's grief process better or worse than anyone else's. It's just different.

CHAPTER 35
ROLES OF FAMILY MEMBERS

Being A Decision Maker/Durable Power of Attorney

What does being a decision maker actually mean?

In the world of healthcare, there is an extremely important legal document we ask every person to fill out during a hospital stay, signing up for home health or hospice service and many other areas of healthcare.

That's the Durable Power of Attorney (DPOA), specific to healthcare decision-making. A financial power of attorney is a different form with differing requirements that won't be addressed here. Please see an attorney or legal service for that document. Here is a link to a free DPOA form at the time of this publication.

The person who is your DPOA is someone you choose, and someone you trust with your life. That's not an exaggeration. The person, or people, you designate as your decision maker(s)s must be strong enough to carry out your wishes, *not theirs*, and not buckle under the pressure other family members may put on them.

Remember: these are your decisions. The DPOA is carrying out decisions you've already made, will make soon, or are decisions they think *you would choose* for yourself should you unexpectedly be unable to.

This could happen in the event of a catastrophic car crash, a stroke, heart attack or other sudden event that has incapacitated you. (Again, get this done early so no one has to be in the extremely stressful situation of having to decide things for you. This applies to all of us as we never know what can happen or when).

This license (DPOA) to make decisions you've given to someone else only goes into effect when you are in a condition that prevents you from making your own decisions. *It does not give this person license to take over your life against your wishes.*

An example of this would be: you're getting your end-of-life business done, but are of sound mind and body, you're just preparing for the end of your life at some time in the distant future. The person you've named as DPOA *can't* come in and override your decisions. They *can't* take over your life. (I just said that, but it bears repeating). If someone tries that, you've picked the wrong DPOA and need to make changes ASAP.

This document can easily and quickly be changed, updated or revoked at any time, just by tearing up the document. You can then quickly name another, more suitable, person as your DPOA.

Sometimes, mostly older women in traditional households, or certain cultures, will defer all decision-making to their oldest son, rather than making the decision on their own. That works for their situation but doesn't work for everyone. Do what works for you.

CHAPTER 36
THE BEST AND THE WORST

Approaching end-of-life is a time that brings out the best and the worst in people, and I am not kidding about that in any way. People in your family (and sometimes people not in your family) may come out of the woodwork to try to tell your children what they should be doing and how they should be doing it, causing a lot of chaos, and then leave.

I call these people Bomb Droppers. They aren't involved in your life much and can live at a distance or be close by. When you've let it be known you're on hospice they come to visit you, boss you or your family around, and demand to know why you aren't doing chemo, or hydration or any other thing they can think of.

They cause the trouble they intended to (Yes, it's deliberate. It's always deliberate.) and then they leave, sometimes never being heard from again, or they can continue to cause problems for you and your family until someone, you or your DPOA, stops them from their bad behavior.

You're under no obligation to allow these people (or

anyone, really) into your home or your loved one's home, just because you're related to them by blood or have been friends for decades. Visitors must behave themselves, keep their opinions to themselves, and if they can't, then they aren't allowed to see you (or your loved one if you're the DPOA) or have any input whatsoever. It's that simple.

That's not being mean or harsh, that's protecting yourself and/or your family member from people who aren't there to be helpful.

You already know who this is in your family after reading the above description, don't you? (Yes, them!) That cousin, or aunt, or sibling who just *has to cause drama* wherever they go, and you have to brace yourself for their visits. (You're nodding as you read this, knowing exactly who I'm talking about, aren't you?)

Stopping these people is a task that may fall to the DPOA if, or when, you're unable to uphold boundaries with people around you.

Having boundaries is necessary for all of us in every situation, but most especially at the end of our lives. Many of us were taught as children to be nice or polite and allow other people to walk all over us. You can still be nice and firmly uphold your boundaries.

Remember: The people having issues with your boundaries are the ones who are violating them! So, unfortunately, you do have to keep an eye on certain family members who may act in ways that aren't in your best interest.

You have a limited amount of time left. Do you really want to spend it dealing with drama and chaos? I hope your answer is a definite no.

When The DPOA Takes Effect

When the DPOA kicks in/takes effect and you're either unconscious or deemed unable to make your own decisions, hospice will look to your DPOA for decisions that must be made.

Examples of decisions needing to be made include:

- When to put a urinary catheter in you to keep you dry
- When to stop medications other than comfort meds
- When to stop feeding you
- When to stop trying to give you oral liquids

Your hospice nurse will guide your family and caregivers about these decisions, too.

This DPOA is not a job to be taken on lightly, so if someone doesn't feel they can handle this task effectively then they must step aside and let someone else take over this position for you. There's no judgement about this. If one person can't/won't do it, then you simply select another DPOA.

You can also designate two people, whom you trust, to act in your best interest as well. I personally have my older brother as my DPOA as my son is in his early 20's at the time I'm writing this book. He could do this, but I don't want to put that kind of pressure on him at this time in his life, should the need arise. My brother and I are both designated as DPOA for our mother.

The ideal way for this process to go smoothly is to have all of your decisions made prior to you being unable to do so and have them written in legal documents with copies to several people you trust and to your hospice. It's simple and easy to do, you don't have to pay for an attorney for these, either, so I'm encouraging you to get this done as soon as possible.

CHAPTER 37
DUTIES OF THE PRIMARY CAREGIVER

In this section I'll speak directly to the primary caregivers.

What being the primary caregiver (PCG) means is that you are signing up to be the 24/7 caretaker for your loved one or for the person you've been hired to take care of. This can be very rewarding or drive you over the edge into insanity. Just depends on your personality, physical abilities, whether you can depend on other family members for assistance or think you can do it all on your own. (Hint: You can't do it all alone. You will need help.)

Being the PCG means you'll be cooking, shopping for, feeding, bathing, administering medications, changing the patient's clothing, as well as soiled diapers/clothing if the patient is unable to get out of bed or has significant mobility issues. This includes any release of bowel and bladder that happen between the bed or chair and the bathroom. (Hint: this is where a bedside commode can come in really handy, and hospice will provide one at no charge.)

Hospice doesn't send somebody over to change dirty

diapers. I cannot emphasize that enough. *Hospice does not send someone over to change dirty diapers.* That is the job of the PCG. PCGs can be family members, they can be a hired person, or they can be the staff at an assisted living or nursing home. Hospice care does not have to be at home with you being the 24-hour person if you are unable to do it.

Hospice was designed for patients to be at home in their comfort zone and be cared for by their own family, but there are many options now. When hospice was created, there were few nursing facilities the way there are now, and dying people were sent to hospitals to die, which is the worst place for hospice care. Visiting hours are restrictive and people often died alone. In-home hospice is so much better so people can die in their own homes in peace and surrounded by their loved ones.

Hospice will see the patient wherever they call home. (Except for under a bridge in a cardboard box. A hospice here in Albuquerque tried to provide hospice care for the homeless and let's just say, that didn't work out too well. Noble idea, but not safely doable.)

Back to you as the PCG.

Admittedly, family dynamics vary from family to family, and people work outside the home more now than when this system was designed for in-home care. Our cultures and economies continue to evolve over the decades and hospice will continue to evolve as well.

There have been many articles and much research about whether it's a better death to die at home or in the hospital. Here's a link to one I like in support of a home death. (If you have the paperback book, search: Cancer Council and article: In Your Own Home).

People are much more comfortable in their own

homes and still have access to great care from hospice without the clinical, cold and often-lacking, hospital setting. Hospital nurses and personnel are trained to save people, not offer the best comfort possible while allowing people die naturally. (Hospitals don't want people dying in them because the deaths effect their review numbers and give them poorer performance numbers. This can also affect their reputations and the trust of the community if these numbers are low. Think of it as Yelp ratings for hospitals.)

One downside of being elderly and having an elderly caregiver is that it's simply not possible for everyone to have the experience of an in-home death without extra help. Elderly caregivers are not always capable of carrying out the physical needs of someone at end-of-life. This is where the family and/or hired caregiver needs to be added, because one elderly person can't do it all. (And honestly, one younger caregiver can't do it all, either.)

There are a lot of changes that go on between the time when a person starts hospice care at home and when they actually die. There are many ups and downs and a lot of changes someone will experience (see Stages of Dying in this book.) People must have supervision and physical care during this time.

They aren't capable of caring for themselves. People aren't being deliberately problematic at this time. They really are not capable of good mental processing or taking care of their physical needs at this time. Having a trusted family member or PCG ensures they are safe, clean and comfortable while nature takes its course.

Another area the PCG needs to be comfortable is in administering medications, which includes narcotics and suppositories. (Sorry folks. Whatever medicine goes in the mouth can also go in the rectum and be absorbed just as well.)

Most people don't swallow effectively, or at all, toward the end-of-life. The medications in the Comfort Pack can be absorbed in the mouth so they don't have to be swallowed for the meds to work. These medications can be given to someone who is comatose, and they will work because they are absorbed in the mouth.

The caregiver(s) must be willing to give medications on a regular basis and be willing to give narcotics as well as overcome their own fears, or biases, about the use of narcotics.

Let me address the biggest fear people have about the use of narcotics at end-of-life.

Addiction. There's no such thing as becoming addicted to narcotics on hospice the way someone does who is using street drugs.

When someone is on hospice it's a completely different set of circumstances than somebody who is on the street using street drugs unsupervised and/or uncontrolled or for recreation.

Patients on hospice can become *dependent* on narcotics for pain and symptom control. That is expected, but *it is not addiction* in the way most people think of addiction. There are people around you who have addictions you aren't aware of right now.

- Alcohol
- Sugar
- Caffeine
- Gambling
- Food
- Shopping

- Love
- Anger/Rage
- Sex
- Video Games
- Internet Use

All of the above, and many more things, can be addictions as well as the illicit drugs we hear about on the news. I'm not talking about those.

Very specifically, I'm addressing narcotic use with people who are dying AND receiving hospice care under the care of a hospice physician. That is as safe as it can be.

We don't have any hospice patients knocking over liquor stores to support their drug habits. There aren't any little old lady hospice patients buying drugs on street corners. As silly as those examples are, I use them because they really demonstrate the difference between hospice patients and people looking for drugs on the street.

Hospice controls the amount of all medications dispensed at one time, including narcotics. The reason for this is many hospice patients change quickly, which means they could require more medication or a lot less. (When someone dies, they don't need meds any longer, and hospices waste a phenomenal amount of medications at the time of death.)

Reminder: The hospice pharmacy will dispense only 2 weeks of medications at a time because doses frequently need to be changed (increased or decreased) or the patient dies. The 2-week rule is a Medicare regulation, not pharmacies or your hospice being stingy with meds.

On occasion there is diversion in the home, which means a family member, caregiver, friend or visitor, is *stealing narcotics from the patient.* Hospice staff are required to report this theft to the police as it falls under the category of elder abuse, and your family member, or caregiver, could be arrested for this theft. Here's a link to an article about theft of narcotics at end-of-life.

There are measures hospices take to prevent medication theft, but we can't prevent it 100% without your help. If the patient's PCG or a family member is drug seeking, meaning *they are using the medications they steal or selling them*, then hospice will not provide more medications while this person is in the home. Hospice is not that person's drug supplier and if someone in your home is stealing your medications, you don't want that person responsible for your care, either.

That may sound harsh, but hospice will not provide narcotics in an unjustified and illegal manner to anyone. Hospices are responsible to Medicare and must follow the regulations or they will be out of business.

That was a lot of information on medications and narcotics, but it's a very important subject, and you must understand this before you become the PCG.

What else do you have to do as the PCG?
Decision Making

THE PCG and the Durable Power of Attorney (DPOA) for making decisions is often the same person but doesn't have to be. You can be the DPOA and someone else can be the PCG.

Hopefully, the patient has made all their decisions about treatments and death prior to this point, or will soon, with the guidance of the hospice team.

If the family member you're caring for hasn't made these decisions, *you will be expected to make them.*

This includes whether or not to perform CPR (please say no), funeral arrangements (burial or cremation and which mortuary to use), what cemetery to be buried in and many other details.

Are you up to the task of making these decisions, even if you don't like it? Are you willing to set aside your emotions and feelings to make choices that are right for the person you're caring for?

If you can't do these things, that's okay. Simply step aside as the PCG and let someone else do it, or have someone else be the decision maker (durable POA) and you can do the hands-on care.

There are many ways to accomplish these tasks needed by your loved one. You will need to modify them for your individual situation.

Remember: if it's not working for you, you *can* make changes to this designation at any time. If you become ill or move away or for any number of reasons, you can, and should, bow out as the PCG and have it assigned to someone else.

There is no shame in saying you can't do it or aren't willing to do it. It's as simple as yes, you can, or no, you can't.

Hospice will help you figure it out.

You don't have to do it by yourself.

CHAPTER 38

OTHER TYPES OF
HOSPICE CARE

Respite: What It Is and How to Get It

Medicare understands that caregiving is an exhausting experience, and no one can do it without a break. Respite is a *planned time for the caregiver to rest*, not for an emergency. (We really don't have emergencies in hospice the way there are emergencies in other areas of healthcare.)

Reasons for respite can be that the caregiver needs a break. Maybe they've got the 'flu or must have knee surgery, or any number of things, and need time off from being the PCG for a few days.

Respite is a 5-day stretch of time where the patient will be taken to a care-home in their area, or if they're fortunate enough to be with a hospice that has its own in-patient unit, you or your loved one can go there for the 5 days. They will be cared for by the nursing staff 24/7 and at the end of the 5 days they will be returned home to you, and you carry on as before.

Occasionally, the respite break makes you as the PCG

realize how exhausted you are and that 5 days off isn't enough. We encourage you to really take this break as it's designed and not go to the facility where your loved one is and stay there all day. That's *not* a break.

During this break you may also realize you need more help than you thought. This is where your hospice social worker can become very helpful to you with community resources and/or bringing in other family members to help on a scheduled basis so that one person isn't bearing the entire load of caregiving.

Sometimes, the patient on respite will have what we call *a change in condition* and enter the transitional phase of dying while on respite. That's okay. It happens. It doesn't mean that anything is wrong, but it is a change.

Sometimes a person needs to be away from their family in order to let go. We just never know until it happens. Your hospice team will help guide you through what happens next.

If your loved one can't get in the car for the family to transport them to the facility for respite, the hospice will make arrangements for a *non-emergency ambulance* to transport them to the respite facility. And hospice covers the cost of the ambulance transport.

<u>Remember</u>: the ambulance transport is arranged by hospice, paid for by hospice, but is *not an emergent situation*. Don't call 911 for a respite stay. It won't happen that way and your loved one will be returned home to you. There are processes that need to be followed to set it up and there needs to be room at the facility for your loved one.

How Often Can You Have Respite?

A respite can be arranged once every certification

period. The first 2 certification periods are 90-days each, then in 60-day increments thereafter.

If you are interested in having a respite scheduled, contact your hospice nurse or social worker and they will handle all the details.

I do suggest take this opportunity to rest and regroup. You'll be a better caregiver if you take care of yourself, too.

General In-Patient (GIP)

Another reason someone might be taken to an in-patient unit is for symptoms, usually pain, not controlled in the home.

Hospice takes the patient to their own hospice in-patient unit, or a nursing facility, with the intention to make rapid medication changes that can't be done in the home. The plan is to get the symptoms quickly under control, then return the patient to their home on the new medication schedule and resume home hospice care. There may be new medications, or higher doses of current medications, but you as the PCG and/or DPOA will be updated on these changes.

The intention, whether respite or symptom management, is *always to return the patient home*, not keep them in the in-patient unit for any longer than necessary. Again, Medicare rules.

Psychosis is someone is having out of control mental conditions is an exception, and they may have to go to a psychiatric facility, or unit, until the behavior and medications are both adjusted, then they can return home.

Residential Hospice Houses

Some states have hospice houses where patients can live out their days cared for by hospice staff. This is fantastic and needed very much, but there are simply not enough of them. Each state is different, and you'll have to research that information on your own for your state. The state of New Mexico, where I live, doesn't have any residential hospice houses.

CHAPTER 39

OTHER SHORT-TERM REASONS FOR HOSPICE

There are some non-cancer, acute (short and fast) reasons that hospice can be called in for and have different guidelines. We term those cases as *sudden events* when the patient isn't expected to recover from the situation. They can happen to anyone at any time, but all are unexpected and catastrophic.

This person isn't going to survive.

Examples are:

- Cardiac Arrest
- Catastrophic stroke
- Acute Kidney Failure
- Car wrecks with significant brain and/or bodily injury
- Seizures with brain injury
- Falls with brain injury

Some of these conditions can be survivable, depending on the person, their age and circumstances. What I'm referring to here are the catastrophic events when a person isn't going to survive this sudden and deadly event, no matter what sort of medical intervention is provided.

Hospice gets involved when the person isn't expected to survive and has chosen, or their family chosen for them, comfort care only.

Usually, the person has already been taken to a hospital for care and the family has been given the devastating news that their loved one isn't going to survive the injury.

Strokes and heart attacks are injuries to the brain and heart muscle, though it seems odd to think of them in that way.

My younger brother, as related earlier in this book, had a devastating brain injury at age 55. He had a stroke to the brain stem, which is where all the necessary functions required to run the body, such as breathing, swallowing, etc. are contained. When that area of the brain is injured, there is no coming back from it with any quality of life. He could have been kept alive in a nursing home, connected to an artificial life support respirator and artificial tube feedings that would have required surgery to put a tube into this stomach. He would then have been susceptible to aspiration (inhaling) of the tube feedings into his lungs, developed multiple infections, serious bedsores and been tortured this way for years. (And yes, it is torture.) He would not have been able to communicate because he'd have had to have the respirator attached to a hole (tracheostomy) in his neck designed for this.

That is not living. That is extensive torture and suffering.

And that is why we all need to have our end-of-life decisions made well ahead of time.

Aside from a car crash, a catastrophic event such as what my brother experienced is generally *not* just one thing. If it had been just the stroke, my brother might have survived, but with all the other illnesses he had on top of it, the stroke was not survivable.

Catastrophic events are another excellent reason to have your end-of-life business completed well ahead of time.

Please take this urgent task out of the hands of your family and make your decisions now. Give your family the gift of being prepared.

Some hospitals have their own hospice units which is wonderful for patients and families. That's called hospital hospice. The patient remains in the hospital, but in a special care unit until they die and are cared for by hospice nurses.

CHAPTER 40
GENERAL IN-PATIENT HOSPITAL HOSPICE

This section may be more complicated than you need right now, so feel free to skip ahead to the next section.

Sometimes it's not possible to transfer a patient from the ICU to a separate hospice unit, so the patient remains in the ICU or wherever they are in the hospital, and hospice is brought in as a secondary layer of care. The ICU nurses still care for the patient, but the hospice nurse helps to guide the comfort care.

This is also called GIP General In-Patient, as previously explained, but a different type of GIP.

In this day and age of reviews, ratings and statistics hospital systems are very concerned about how hospital deaths will affect their review scores and ratings in many areas. Hospitals get negative dings when there are deaths in the hospital. By bringing hospice in for a patient who's going to die soon, but is unable to be moved elsewhere, the hospital avoids a negative hit on their statistics by moving the patient's death score to the hospice outside the hospital where it isn't an issue. Rather than the patient death counting against a hospital, the hospital shifts the responsibility for the death to a hospice. With hospice, the mortality rates do not count negatively, because everyone is expected to die on hospice.

For boring, but kind of interesting, statistics, check Morbidity and Mortality Report Weekly.

Just to break things up a little:

QUESTION: What do you think the number 1 cause of preventable death is in the United States and possibly the world?

Hint: it's not heart disease, cancer or car crashes.

Answer: here.

Now, back to the fascinating topic of hospital statistics.

In 2008 Medicare made a significant change to their reimbursement of hospital costs. Medicare would no longer pay for hospital-acquired infections, errors and many other things. See that article . As a result, hospitals have had to become creative to keep their statistics on unexpected deaths low, as described above. Diverting some of these death to hospice for short, catastrophic deaths helps. It's kind of a cheat, but it's done extensively.

The Biggest Benefit to Hospital Hospice

By bringing in hospice before the patient dies, the family receives the emotional support they need during the crisis and hospice still provides grief support to the family for a year after the patient dies.

126

If the people who experienced a sudden event/death weren't able to be admitted to hospice, the family wouldn't be able to receive grief support from hospice. It's worth admitting someone to GIP, or the hospice unit, for the family to have this essential benefit. When something traumatic, unexpected and fast happens, the family hasn't had time to adjust to the changes. GIP gives them a little buffer of time.

Sometimes these families include small children because the patient is a 40-year-old man who suffered a heart attack and has died or was in a car accident and is expected to die soon. Those families need all the support they can get.

CHAPTER 41

IS A SLOW OR QUICK DEATH BETTER?

A fter all the years I've been a hospice nurse (27 years and counting) I still haven't been able to decide whether a quick death or a longer illness is better for families.

With a quick death the length of time someone will experience their illness is obviously much shorter. A longer illness gives the family more time to adjust to, and plan for, a life without this person.

At the same time, watching someone you love go through the process of treatment, declining, wasting away, and eventually dying is a much harder thing to experience. It is different person to person and family to family.

The Dying Time

In this section, I'll explain in detail many of the signs, symptoms, changes and behaviors someone can experience, or you as the caregiver, will observe in your loved one as they get closer to their death.

You can experience some or all of these changes and not

in any particular order. As each of us is a unique individual, so is our dying experience going to be unique. Everybody's disease process, their spirit, their desire to stay (live) or their desire to leave (die) is different. It depends on which one is stronger. When people say they're too tired to stay, or they are being called "home," they leave faster.

When people say they want to go "home," they are referring to their spiritual home, not the physical house they have lived in. In spirit, they are ready to die.

So, what happens when you're getting ready to die? Keep reading and I'll explain.

Changes and symptoms you may experience or see:

Sundowning

Families have reported to me that their loved one has been cooking in the middle of the night, or cleaning the house, wanting up to the bathroom 15 times, or a variety of tasks in the middle of the night that are absolutely unnecessary and can often be dangerous if someone is unsupervised. This syndrome is not limited to people with a dementia diagnosis. It can occur to anyone.

Medications that help override stimulation of the brain at night is essential. At this point naturopathic treatment, such as Melatonin, are generally not enough to keep a person down. Episodes of sundowning syndrome requires heavy-duty medications prescribed by the hospice doctor. This medication is essential to keep the patient asleep, but may require a few dose adjustments to get the dose that works. Heavy medication is essential for the patient to be safe, but it's also essential for the caregiver to be able to sleep, too.

The caregiver cannot function well if they're exhausted

from sleep deprivation because the patient's been up every night for five for six hours. The patient will awaken at some time during the day and have no memory of what has gone on all night.

It's very frustrating to the family for this to go on and they often don't understand why Grandma is up at 3 AM cleaning the kitchen. She's not doing it on purpose. She can't help it. We never can predict who was going to experience sundowning syndrome until it happens.

This is where communication with your nurse is essential for you to report changes in behavior to the nurse so that the nurse can help you understand why this is going on and get medications ordered quickly. Your nurse also keeps the entire team updated about the patient's condition and behaviors.

Sleeping More

When people keep to their nightly routine and start taking naps in the afternoon where they never did before, becomes concerning to families. That's okay, they're listening to their body. When the body is tired and needs to rest, I highly recommend a nap. And that includes you as the caregiver, too.

When the patient sleeps or naps the caregiver should, too.

In essence, you have a giant toddler in your home and when they sleep it's essential that you sleep as well.

Loss of interest in activities

That's a big one. For families, this is a change that can be clearly identified. Family see the patient as changing significantly when they no longer are interested in reading, or gardening, or sewing, or whatever activity they have engaged in for years is no longer of interest to them.

Sometimes it's because pain is not controlled well enough, and the pain interferes someone's ability to engage in anything. Always check with the patient and the hospice nurse to make sure that the patient is as comfortable as possible without too much medication. Some people will choose to have more pain and be more awake. Other people choose more medication and sedation to be more comfortable with the pain process and sacrifice their awake time. That is an individual decision for the family and the patient to make together. There are certain disease processes that are more painful than others. That is something that your nurse will help educate you about. Bone cancer and pancreatic cancer are two of the most painful diseases and often require heavy pain medications. Dementia and Alzheimer's Disease are not known for pain.

Loss of appetite

Families often fear that their loved one is going to lose weight and be malnourished, or starve to death, during the dying process. It's inevitable, but you shouldn't be afraid of this or let it make you anxious. The patient will lose weight. They will be malnourished, but not starving to death. What's causing their decline and death is the disease process, which causes poor appetite. Loss of appetite and weight loss are part of the natural dying process related to many different diagnoses. As we age, our intestinal tract is less efficient than it used to be, so it doesn't absorb nutrients in the same way that a younger person does.

Sometimes nutritional supplements help the family feel

better about the weight loss. High protein shakes are fine to give someone as long as the person can drink them without choking.

First, ask yourself if you're insisting they eat/drink for you or for themselves? Are you making yourself feel better by feeding them as you're trying to delay the emotional pain you know you'll experience when your loved one dies?

By keeping someone's body alive longer you may be prolonging the inevitable and prolonging the suffering. You're not giving them more quality of life, only more suffering. When someone reaches this point in their dying time, you can't change it, and you can't walk back the clock to buy more time. You're only prolong the suffering. I know that is a hard thing to read, to think about, and to apply to your own situation, but at this point you have to. You're reading this book for a reason, whether you purchased it or someone gave it to you. Though this is tough, this is information that's essential for you to understand right now.

If hungry, people will eat. They are listening to their bodies at this time and naturally reducing calories and fluids to ensure an easier death. When someone turns away from the food, or pushes it away, that means they don't want it and you need to listen to them. Coercing someone into eating isn't helping anyone.

Remember earlier in the book the quote I gave from a hospice doctor I worked with? I'll repeat it here, because it's worth repeating and remembering: Feeding someone, giving IV fluids for hydration and other life-prolonging measures don't prolong life. What they do is prolong the suffering.

Are you prolonging the suffering of your loved one? Does your loved one want to drink the supplements or are you giving them as a way to delay your own grief process?

Only you can answer that question. I encourage you to sit with this thought a while and see what comes up for you.

Breathing Changes

Most people will experience some sort of breathing changes as they are approaching the actively dying time as well as the imminently dying phase.

Shallow respirations, change in the pattern and even absence of breathing are all observed and expected at this time, from when someone is in the transitional phase to when they ultimately die. There may also be an increase in lung and mouth secretions because the patient isn't swallowing normally. There is a medication in the Comfort Pack to help with this.

Questions to ask yourself now and check in with yourself in the future.

Does my loved one have quality of life, or are they merely existing?

Why do you want to keep someone alive in this condition?

Why aren't you letting them go?

If you observed this situation in someone else's home, what would you think of it?

When do you think it's okay for someone to die?

How badly do they need to suffer before you'll let them go?

How old do they have to be before they're allowed to die?

I know this is painful, and I'm sorry for that pain.

Watching someone decline and die is an emotionally painful process to go through for yourself or a loved one. I understand that, and my heart goes out to you.

Dying is the only part of living that's inevitable and we do our best to get through it.

A Unique and Possibly Last Opportunity

Relationships can be difficult and have lots of history behind them. Being in hospice is an opportunity to heal some aspects of your relationships with your parents, or if you are the parent, with your children. Those who are left behind can benefit from healing now as there won't be another time for this. Sometimes, it only takes saying I'm sorry for the healing to begin.

The Dying Time-The One-Way Street

Ongoing need for pain medication during this end-of-life process is necessary.

In hospice, it's essential to continue to medicate a person who is unconscious, non-verbal and can't communicate. People near death are not able to tell us with words if they're uncomfortable, so we have to read the signals they do give us, called non-verbal communication, and medicate periodically so there's always a little medication in the system.

If someone has been on long-term pain medications, it's essential to continue to give those medications on a regular basis. If unmedicated, the patient will have periods of extreme pain that will take much longer to get controlled and use a lot more medication than if the patient is medicated periodically, every 4 to 6 hours, during the last few days of life.

Skin Breakdown

This is common, especially under a few certain circumstances.

When patients urinate in a brief, (or adult diaper) and the brief is not changed frequently, this sets up the person for skin breakdown in the folds of their groin, buttocks and any place where there is pressure, such as on their hip bones. The areas at the highest risk for skin breakdown are: the back of the head, shoulder blades, elbows, tailbone, hips and heels.

The biggest reason somebody experiences skin breakdown is from pressure on the skin. Pressure occurrs when a person lies in the same position in the bed, or sitting on their chair for extended periods of time as well as wrinkled sheets beneath someone. Just about anything can cause pressure.

We, in healthcare, used to think that skin breakdown only occurred when patients were left for hours and hours or days in the same position and not repositioned. Over the last 10 years there have been scientific discoveries report breakdown can happen in a matter of hours. That's why it's so important for people to be repositioned with assistance, if they can't do it themselves.

Your nurse and the home health aide will show you how to reposition somebody in bed and even how to change the sheets of someone who can't get out of bed. Even somebody who isn't in pain, but lying in bed without moving their joints and muscles, can become uncomfortable. The recommendation, or best practice, is to reposition every 2 to 4 hours and that's generally enough for most people.

Skin breakdown happens in four stages. The fourth stage is the most severe and can be down to the bone, exposing the muscle and is foul smelling.

The only things that cans heal wound like that are massive amounts of calories which most of our patients are incapable of taking in, reduction in pressure, which means repositioning and turning and time. The goal in hospice is to try to keep the wound from getting worse, but it's unlikely that someone with that kind of serious wound will heal that wound.

Due to immobility and weight loss many patients are susceptible to skin breakdown to some degree, and we will do our best to help you prevent that.

Another area of skin breakdown that occurs is called Kennedy Terminal Ulcers. (Again, named after a doctor named Kennedy).

These sores are different in nature than sores called Decubitus Ulcers. Kennedy sores can happen in areas that are not in a pressure area they can occur on the top of a hip or a thigh and we never know who's going to develop them and who is not. They usually develop within a few days of dying and the cause is unknown.

Another very common skin change you may see is called mottling. This is a pinkish-red splotchy discoloration that is usually observe first on the soles of the feet, the palms of the hands and the knees. Sometimes mottling will extend from the toes all the way up to the hips and this modeling is an indication that the circulation is changing significantly. Some people never develop it all, and sometimes we see it just on the tip of the nose or the knees. This skin discoloration is not painful or uncomfortable and usually when we see the mottling it's when the person is no longer awake and is deep within, doing their end-of-life work.

Kidneys, Liver and Bowels

URINE OUTPUT, the amount of urine the kidneys make in a day, slows down as someone approaches death. Urine will become rusty, or dark red, in color and sometimes foul smelling. This is not the sign of a bladder infection. This is a sign of kidney failure which is not uncomfortable. People who die from kidney failure usually go to sleep and have an uneventful passing.

The other organ that stops working and can cause orange discoloration of the urine is the liver. When the liver fails, the urine can turn a very dark orange.

The bowels/intestines slow down as disease progresses, sometimes months ahead of time. Our intestines are stimulated by activity, hydration and bulk of food. Most people at end-of-life are lacking in all three of these areas, so the intestines become sluggish. Certain medications used for pain can also cause constipation. This is why hospice nurses gets nosy about their patient's bowel movements. It's quite a necessary thing for the nurse to know to prevent constipation from becoming severe.

Visions

PEOPLE HAVE visions of the other side and often see the spirits of dead loved ones, angels, animals, children and a variety of different things that we don't see. Just because we don't see the things our loved one does, doesn't mean they're not present. That sounds convoluted and not meant to be. The things people see are very real to the person having the vision. There is a lot that we don't know and understand about the dying process. I think that these answers are reserved for us when our time comes to die.

These visions are not hallucinations related to schizo-phrenia or other mental illness, high fevers, poisoning or many other causes. People who are not on any medications still have visions of dead loved ones and a variety of things toward end-of-life.

One of my first hospice patients (a really long time ago) was getting close to her dying time. She was still verbal, but kept her eyes closed a lot. One day when I was visiting her, she was batting invisible stuff away from her head, wiping stuff off of her face and there was nothing that her daughter or I could see. Her daughter asked what she was doing, and she said, "There are rose petals falling on me."

Rose petals. What a beautiful image for the daughter to have of rose petals floating down on her mother, even though she couldn't see them.

Anxiety and Pre-Terminal Anxiety

THESE TWO CHANGES often come up with people getting closer to their dying time. Regular anxiety can be due to many reasons, such as dementia, medication changes, lack of sleep or dehydration and can be experienced at any time in someone's disease process.

This type of anxiety or restlessness can be comforted by the use of an anti-anxiety medication from the Comfort Kit. If you're not sure what to use, call the hospice or your nurse and they will direct you on what to do.

Pre-Terminal Anxiety is a different kind of anxiety and specifically occurs 2-4 days prior to someone's death.

THE DYING PROCESS IS NOT ENTIRELY SCIENTIFIC
AND NOT WELL UNDERSTOOD. THERE ARE
SPIRITUAL ASPECTS OF THE DYING PROCESS THAT
WE'RE NOT PRIVY TO AT THIS POINT AND I THINK
IS RESERVED FOR EACH OF US WHEN OUR TIME
COMES TO TRANSITION TO THE OTHER SIDE.

We generally see some agitation in people prior to death
and if severe we call it preterminal agitation. This agitation
can be confusing at first.

The patient is up in their chair, they want back in bed.
They want something. No, they don't want that. Make me
this. Why did you make me that? I need this, no I don't
want that! They're just not comfortable any place, chair or
bed. They're restless in the bed, so they want up in the
chair. When they're in the chair they want back in the bed.
It's this type of behavior for a few days and is seemingly
endless.

This is not an expression or indication of pain. This is
different and is a sign that there is an unresolved issue,
emotional or spiritual, that needs to be dealt with prior to
this person being able to die. This is the wrestling of the
issue that they are going through internally as they process
the issue and let go of it, that we see externally as pre-
terminal agitation.

Not everybody experiences this, and we never know
who will until they manifest the pre-terminal anxiety.

Another sign that this is pre-terminal anxiety is that the
normal anti-anxiety medications aren't as effective. The
reason is that this is a spiritual or emotional issue, not a
physical issue and the only way to solve the issue is by
allowing your loved one to go through this pre-terminal
anxiety without interference.

It's definitely exhausting emotionally and physically for the caregivers as they tend to the patient. Please be assured that this phase will end, and your loved one will come out of it, but they must go through this process as it's an essential part of the dying process. We can't medicate someone out of this or do this part for them.

People with controlling personalities have a harder time letting go and generally will have pre-terminal agitation. People with controlling personalities are usually associated with diseases like heart disease, COPD (emphysema) or other lung diseases. If you, or your loved one, have any of those illnesses just know it could be a rocky ride.

Our job at this time, including the caregiver and the nurse, is to keep your loved one comfortable and safe while this phase goes on.

This means you may end up having to give much higher doses of medications for anxiety and it probably won't make the symptoms go away. That is anticipated in this phase. One reason we give additional medications is for safety as the patient isn't as capable of good judgement getting in and out of bed frequently and above all, we want them to be safe during this phase.

Pre-Terminal Agitation generally goes away, or resolves, within 24 to 48 hours. After the end of the pre-terminal agitation phase, people will usually die within a few days.

The reason people die soon after this pre-terminal agitation phase is that they've resolved the last thing that has kept them from letting go and passing to the other side.

Often, we never know what that issue is as it's deeply personal to the person who is experiencing it.

Patient Story:

When I was working in the in-patient unit, we had a female patient who was taking her last breath, but she stopped her dying process. She opened her eyes and said, "I can't go yet. I'm still so mad at my husband." It was about an issue that had occurred over 40 years prior. She and her husband talked about it, they resolved the issue, and she laid down and died.

Our spirit has imminent power in the strength to stay attached to the body or in the power of letting go of the body and dying. I've seen people die simply because they've decided to do so. They have had enough of this life, the lay down and die. Other people live way longer than expected, simply because they aren't ready to leave.

This occurs across all cultures, all faiths, or no faith. This because there is a spirit inhabiting the body. This is a spiritual issue that we as spirits must resolve before we can let go.

Patient Story: Man From China

THE LONGEST I'VE personally seen anyone linger without nourishment or water, including IV fluids, was 6 weeks. An incredible, 6 weeks!

In our in-patient unit we were caring for a gentleman from mainland China who had moved to be closer to his children, then he developed colon cancer.

During this phase he was what we could consider to be comatose. We administered comfort medications, but he had no other source of nutrition or fluids. When we would turn him, bathe him or do any care, he would fight us, become very rigid and resistant to what we were doing. When we finished our tasks, then he relaxed and was in his comatose state again. He had no IV for hydration, yet his kidneys continued to function for this entire time.

This was an astonishing length of time for someone to survive this way. The conclusion I eventually came to was that he had a spirit that wasn't ready to let go of his body yet.

Sometimes the power of the spirit is so strong that people who are in the end phase of dying do come back for a little while because their family isn't ready to let go of them.

Patient Story: Daddy Don't Go

ONE EXPERIENCE I observed was an elderly man in his 90s taking his last breath with the family gathered all around him. One of his daughters flung herself over his body (not kidding) crying out, "Daddy don't go! Don't go!" He started to breathe again and stayed in that state for several more hours, much longer than if the daughter had just allowed him to pass without interfering.

The Waiting & Watching Time

Though well-meaning, the family can interfere in the dying process. There's not as much to do for your loved one, but be present, watchful (not anxious) and perform the minimum necessary tasks. Your loved one is deep within, finishing the final phase of their dying and it's a delicate time for them.

At this time, I recommend a hands-off approach, which may seem counterintuitive.

People need someone with them when they die, don't

they? Not always. Families want to touch, do things for, and be with their loved one as they are dying, but a simple touch may be enough to pull someone out of their process.

I suggest sitting with your loved one, being present, peaceful, quiet and loving. Just not touching. This is also not the time to try to get someone to wake up and talk or to eat, drink or take medications. That time has gone. If there is someone in the family, or friends, who can't abide by this suggestion, then they need to be asked to leave or at least step away from the patient.

Some people need an extra bit of privacy to let go. If your loved one seems to be lingering and you've had a bedside vigil, try sitting outside the room, giving them an extra bit of privacy.

Family members have often said that they'd been sitting with their loved one for days, then they went to get a cup of coffee or go to the bathroom and their loved one died during that short period of time.

That was deliberate.

The person just needed an extra bit of privacy to let go. Sometimes family members get upset that they weren't present for their loved one's last breath. I understand from their perspective, this is a loss. From the patient's perspective they needed the privacy. Consider it a last gift from them that you didn't see them take their last breath.

Patient Story: Trying To Die

Next is another experience I had with a patient who was in his 70s. I got a call that the family reported he had fallen out of his wheelchair and stop breathing but they shook him and he started breathing again. They wanted the night nurse to come check him.

When I got to the patient home, he was sitting up in his wheelchair, he was completely rational, he was talking and appropriate. After listening to the family re-tell the story of what had happened and checking his vital signs, I came to a conclusion. I told him that I thought he had tried to die that evening. He said, "yeah, I think so, too." After answering the family's questions, we got him into his bed and settled for the night.

I asked the family to call if they were any other changes, and I left to go home. Approximately 15 minutes later I got a call from the family again, and he had died.

I returned to the house and did the pronouncement of death, educated the family about everything that would happen next, and helped them understand what had happened earlier in the evening. They were very grateful for the earlier visit and felt like they were better prepared for when he did die shortly thereafter.

Some people take the dying process for a test drive is the best way I can describe this.

Patient Story: Taking Death For A Test Drive

I WAS ASKED to admit an elderly female patient in her 90's at her home. The family was afraid she was dying because she had been in bed and unresponsive for three days. She hadn't eaten. She hadn't had anything to drink. She just went to bed one night and didn't wake up for three days. I arrived at the patient's house about five o'clock in the evening, when my shift started. I walked into the home and one family member led me to the kitchen where the patient was sitting up at the table drinking a cup of coffee! Not kidding.

When asked how she felt she said she felt fine. She was

a little hungry, but she was fine and wanted to know what all the fuss was about.

She had no explanation as to why she was out for 3 days.

The only conclusion I've come to after seeing this countless times over the years is that the spirit leaves the body for a while and goes to visit the other side in anticipation of their dying time. Once satisfied with that visit they come back and reanimate their body for a short time which could be a number of days or a few weeks. There is no other explanation for why they would be unresponsive for days at a time and then wake up again and be just fine. At least that's how it's happened in my experience.

When Somebody is Trying to Die

THAT SEEMS LIKE AN ODD STATEMENT, doesn't it? *Trying to die.* Let me explain what that means. Sometimes people are getting ready to let go and pass, but their spirit is still just a little too attached to their body for that to happen. We see this happening in the preterminal agitation phase when someone is trying to get up repeatedly, but fall back onto the bed, because their body isn't physically able to support their weight any longer. Their legs give out from under them, and they collapse on the floor or the bed, but they're still trying to rise. This is why it's so important to medicate someone during the agitation phase. We don't want them to fall and break something important just hours before they die. That would be devastating for them and their family.

CHAPTER 42

A WORD ABOUT FALLS IN THE ELDERLY

Falls are not normal and can cause devastating injuries that lead to death.

Falls happen frequently in the elderly (and that's technically anyone over 65 years old) for a variety of reasons. One of those reasons is that the patient may have an undiagnosed bladder infection or UTI. In younger people the

symptoms of a bladder infection are burning with urination, frequency and often inability to urinate. The urine may smell really bad and have an unusual color.

But not in the elderly! The elderly don't have those same sensations. Often the first sign of a bladder infection in the elderly is an increase in falls. Falls are devastating for people in this age and frail time of their lives.

One serious fall could be devastating and can lead to a person's death. The Office of the Medical Investigator, OMI, is the jurisdiction over all deaths. States may name this office differently, such as the coroner. If a patient falls, sustains a major injury and they die within a certain time frame, generally 6 weeks, hospice is legally obligated to notify OMI at the time of the patient's death. OMI may want to do an investigation or autopsy and investigate why the person fell, what were the circumstances, was something suspicious going on, was emergent care offered to the patient and their family and was the fall the incident that led to this person's death.

You as the family will not be able to stop this process. It's the law and your hospice team is legally obligated to contact OMI.

If there is even the suspicion of a lawsuit in the family, there will be OMI involvement. I once spoke to the family of a patient who had advanced dementia and was still months away from death. The son said, "There are six children and so far, there are six lawyers involved."

Don't be that family. Please.

Hospice and Home Health get very cranky about patient falls. We want to prevent that first big fall because it leads to another fall, and another fall, and another fall. Dying from a fall is not a natural part of life. Patients and families need to be open to hospice staff when suggestions for changes to your home to make it safer for you. Your staff isn't rearranging your home because they think your stuff looks better in another position. This assessment and rearrangement done due to a national mandate, and part of across the USA.

Uncontrolled Pain and Suicide

Uncontrolled pain can unfortunately lead to someone taking their own life. In the many years I've worked in hospice, approximately four patients, at hospices I've worked for, have taken their own lives in violent manners. Their pain had not been controlled well enough and their hospice failed them. It saddens me greatly to think that each of these people thought that suicide was their only option for pain relief.

Suicide is a phenomenon that occurs worldwide and has changed some of the ways in which hospices operate. Patients and their families tire of us asking the same questions every visit, but there are good reasons for those questions. Patient suicide is one of them.

If a person's pain isn't controlled well enough, they will look to end their suffering on their own terms, in ways we wouldn't want them to. Deliberate overdosing or shooting themselves with firearms are the top two ways people end their lives.

All Of the patients I referred to above took their lives in violent ways, and they were all men.

MAID-Medical Aid In Dying.

This procedure is a much more palatable alternative to suicide, but may not be acceptable to some people or their families for a variety of reasons. If the idea of allowing a person to end their suffering and their life on their own terms isn't acceptable to you for any reason, you can skip this section. Just be aware that it is here, and you can come back to it if you wish.

Switzerland has permitted assisted suicide since 1942 under certain circumstances, and several other European countries also permit this procedure.

In the United States, regulations vary state to state, but in general the guidelines include: the person asking for

MAID must be of sound decision-making capacity, be in the end stages of a terminal illness and be physically able to bring a cup of medications to their mouth without assistance and swallow the medications.

Patient Story:

Near the end of last year (2024) I took care of a male patient who had been a college professor, had no particular religious association, and was suffering badly with his illness (cancer) and he was not dying fast enough to his liking.

When I arrived on that Saturday, he had two volumes of Rudyard Kipling positioned near his hand in his bed. They were his best guides to his life and the end of it. They sat silently on the bed waiting to be useful to him. By the look of the covers, they were well-loved books.

On that visit, he asked me about what happened when you died. I said, "Well, that's the million-dollar question, isn't it? No one really knows. We have information from people who have had Near-Death Experiences, but there's no way to validate their stories until you pass over yourself."

I offered to tell him what I knew of how the body ceases function and the things he might experience, or his family might see him go through. The spiritual aspect of his dying would be for him alone to experience.

He pondered what I had said, asked some more questions, which I answered honestly. He said he'd discuss the information I'd given him, and his feelings, with his family and let us (hospice) know what his decision was going to be.

I called and spoke to his wife the next day to check in on him to see if there was anything else I could help him with. She said he was much more peaceful and very excited after the talk we'd had the previous day. I had answered many questions for him and helped him in his decision-making process. She said he talked a lot about that conversation for the rest of the day.

That pleased me as a nurse, and a human, that I could be helpful to someone on such a sensitive topic.

Three days later he died on his own terms.

Hearing that gave me some conflicting emotions. I was happy he was no longer suffering, but at the same time I was sad that such an interesting person had left us.

Each person I care for takes a little bit of me with them but also leaves a little bit of themselves with me to remember them.

Depression in Hospice Patients

This is another area where hospice staff get nosy and ask the same repetitive questions every visit because it's mandated by Medicare and the hospice guidelines. The reason we ask these same questions repeatedly is that depression is common in hospice patients and that can lead to suicide.

Your nurse is assessing every visit whether you, as the patient, or your family observing, are seeing changes that can be concerning. My most recent research indicates that between 25-77% of terminally ill people experience depression. Article here. That's a huge number! It's certainly understandable as we face the end of our lives and evaluate what we have done with it.

We need to go through the phases of grief, and depression is one of those stages. If someone gets stuck in the depression phase, that's where hospice gets concerned and where we can help. Although we can't make the cause of the depression (the disease) go away, we can certainly assist the patient, and their family, understand it, accept it and find ways to cope with the upcoming loss.

I found the statistic of 20% of people who experience untreated depression do commit suicide very sad and discouraging. Not enough is being done to alleviate the suffering in those cases.

Suicide doesn't have to be the answer, but it is the answer for some people. There are ways around and through the depression, such as medications and increased emotional support for you and your family.

Please ask your hospice for help. Don't raise the statistic.

What depression looks like varies from person to person. Some risk factors include:

- Loss of interest in life
- Loss of interest in foods and fluid
- Loss of interest in things that previously brought you joy.
- Sleeping more and for extended periods of time
- Persistent feelings of sadness
- Extreme fatigue or exhaustion
- Thoughts and talk of suicide
- Feelings of helplessness or hopelessness

All those symptoms listed can be attributed to chronic illness as well. That's why it's important for you to connect with your hospice team who are trained in assessing for signs of depression and gauging the risk of suicide.

- No one can do this alone.
- We all need help.
- Sometimes it's just someone to listen to you or sit with you for a while.

CHAPTER 43

PAIN

In hospice we try to alleviate the pain and suffering of our patients. We can't control pain 100% because that disease is on duty 24/7 and medications will only control so much of it.

People often must decide what level of pain they can handle. That's where the pain scale comes in. 1 is mild and 10 is the absolute worst and uncontrolled.

We aim for getting and keeping the pain at a level of 3 or less. For most people that's tolerable and acceptable. They can still function, perform their daily tasks, visit with family and still go on outings without being too sedated by medications.

We can't look at a person and determine their pain level. Pain is whatever someone says it is and at what level it is. If a patient tells me their pain is an 8 out of 10, but they appear to be comfortable and not in serious pain, I have to accept that their pain is an 8 and medicate appropriately. This happens often if a person has had past drug use or alcohol history. They have a tolerance already and require higher doses of pain medications. Your hospice staff will work to keep you comfortable if you fall into that category.

There will be many, many pain medication dose changes and sometimes medication changes as not everyone reacts the same to all medications.

That's why we have more than one medication! The same rule applies to all medications. Sometimes people are super-sensitive to a particular medication that another person doesn't get any benefit from.

An expectation people, and their families, have is that they will be put on a pain medication and that dose will stay the same until they die.

That's not how it works.

Because your disease, such as cancer, continues to change and grow, your medications need to change and adjust, too. Patients are often on extremely high doses of pain medication, because that's the level where their pain is controlled. It has taken many, many months to get to those kinds of levels of pain control and medication adjustments. As the disease changes, so do the medications.

You can expect to have the same kind of medication changes on hospice. This is another reason not to delay hospice care. If you wait until the last few days of your life, hospice doesn't have the time needed to gain control of your pain.

Here is a breakdown of the kinds of pain you may experience.

Pain comes in three areas:

Physical pain: this is where medications are the most helpful. This pain will change over the course of your illness.

Emotional pain: this comes with letting go of your family and this life so you can pass. You have to let go emotionally of your loved ones and things you're attached to.

Spiritual pain: this is a deeply personal kind of pain. Hospice can somewhat help by taking part in chaplain visits or by consulting your spiritual leader. Spiritual pain is the person's area to deal with on their own. As we are all spiritual beings, and have different spiritual beliefs and needs, each person will have a unique experience with it. Some people will have no spiritual pain, which is wonderful.

So, You're on Hospice. Now what?

As much as possible you'll want to get on with living your life. Visit friends. Go out to restaurants. Take trips. Go fishing. Rewatch your favorite movies. Do whatever it is that brings you joy. But don't wait. There will never be a better time than now.

Sometimes people want to go camping again, or go fishing again, or visit their favorite beach and they make it happen.

People often think they should wait until they feel better. Don't wait. Do it now, while you can, even if you're tired. You can always have a nap.

If taking a trip brings you joy or there's someone you want to say goodbye to in person, do it.

I know of a young man who was dying from a rare illness. He essentially threw his own funeral. He had a big party, invited all of his friends, family, anyone he knew. He was able to visit with everyone at once and say his good-byes in a fun, festive atmosphere.

After that, he went to Oregon and ended his life on his own terms. The important part of that story is that he said goodbye to everyone important to him, and everyone got to see him and remember him as a young, happy man.

No one knows how much time any of us have left. Living in the moment, experiencing joy is essential for all of us. If there's someone you're on the outs with and you want to make amends, do it now.

If you're going to travel away from home and go outside the service area of your current hospice, that hospice can help transfer you to another hospice if needed. They will advise you what to do and how to do it, if you experience any difficulties or problems while you're traveling.

This is where communication with your hospice is essential to make sure you have the needed medications and supplies for your trip.

I won't go into details of that here because they can vary from one hospice area to another. Your hospice will guide you through what you need to make your trip happen smoothly.

My recommendation again is don't wait, do it now, whatever it is for you.

Patient Story: Waiting Too Long

One of my patients that passed recently was uncon-scious and approximately within 12 hours of her death when I saw her on a Sunday afternoon. Her son said that one of her wishes was that she wanted to go outside again. Unfortunately, I had to tell him that that was not going to be possible because the bed wouldn't fit through the doors of the assisted living, and she wasn't in a safe condition to be put into a wheelchair and taken outside.

They had waited too long.

I suggested something else.

They could talk to her and describe what they were seeing outside her window. The birds, the trees, the sky and the colors of everything.

The family did take this suggestion, and the patient died peacefully later that evening.

Patient story: The Truck Driver

Another patient I took care of, when I was working in an inpatient hospice unit, was a 42-year-old truck driver with Multiple Myeloma. He was so fatigued by any activity, that he couldn't get out of bed even to sit in a wheelchair. With the slightest activity his oxygen level dropped to dangerous levels.

His greatest desire was to go outside again, but it didn't seem likely that he could do it. One day I got to the inpatient unit and an idea occurred to me. I got a portable oxygen tank and strapped it to the end of his bed. I told him and his family that he was going outside.

Bed and all!

With the family's help, we pushed him down the hall and out the ER doors. We made quite a spectacle.

He was thrilled to be outside and there happened to be a nice shady tree in the parking lot close to the doors. We parked his bed there. His family stayed with him for three or four hours. He enjoyed that so much he was speechless with joy. I was very happy to have helped him accomplish his wish.

There's Always Another Way to Do Something

Sometimes you have to figure things out a little differently than your first impulse, or the way it's always been done. So, if there is something you want to do and your family says you can't do it, or you think you can't do it, look for a different way to accomplish that goal.

Maybe you've seen the Robin Williams movie Patch Adams where the doctor had a patient who had been a big game hunter. One of his last wishes was to go on another game hunt, but he was physically able to do that.

Patch Adams came up with the idea of having *a balloon-animal safari* in the patient's room. That was just delightful to watch. The patient was thrilled with his his big game hunt and was able to die in peace after having one last hunt. If you haven't seen the Patch Adams movie, it's worth a watch. (Warning: Being Robin Williams, there is off-color hilarity, too!)

Walking in Both Worlds

THAT's the term I use for people who are having visions about things that are not seen by the people in the room with them. Although we can't see these things, it doesn't mean they aren't present, and they are very real to the person seeing them.

I took care of a patient in her 60's who was a nurse. It was very interesting to talk with her nurse-to-nurse as she was getting closer to her dying time. She gave me some insight I didn't have at the time, and I really appreciated her perspective.

The last time I saw her she told me about an experience

she had had that morning. She knew she wasn't sleeping, and she knew she wasn't awake. She said she had seen a very beautiful meadow with trees, and birds, and flowers. It was very appealing, and she really wanted to go there, but as she started toward it, it disappeared. She asked what I thought it was that she had seen. I told her I thought <u>that was her other side.</u>

Then she asked me what she should do.

I said, "When it shows up again take another step and see what happens."

She must have done so because she died 3 days later.

On Being Naked

This patient who saw the meadow, was one who needed to be naked in order to pass.

This happens to both men, women, all ages, disease processes and cultures. It's part of the dying process for some people and *not* part of a disease process.

What caregivers may see is their loved one pulling at their clothing or gathering up the sheets into a ball and setting it aside. They may remove their clothing or if they are wearing a patient gown, they'll remove that, as well as their underwear, diaper or brief.

People sometimes need to be naked in order to let go.

Not everybody does this, but if they do it's okay. They're usually in their own home or their own room. If any visitors are offended that's their problem, because this behavior is part of the process for this person who is dying.

It doesn't matter what other people think. This person needs to be naked in order to die. You can tie a sheet to the bedrails over the bed for modesty if you wish. Most of the time people aren't affected by the room temperature. You may struggle trying to keep bedding or clothing on them and at some point, you have to let go of the issue.

What I believe is that the weight of the clothing or the bedding on the body is enough to keep the spirit from leaving. The person needs to remove any impediment to their spirit leaving and clothing or bedding is one of them.

REMEMBER: everything that seems weird is perfectly normal when someone is on hospice.

Temperature Changes

TEMPERATURE CHANGES of the skin include doing from hot to cold, cold to hot, and to the development of a fever are common as the body is shutting down.

These temperature changes are not due to an infection, but due to the brain shutting down and not being to heat or cool the body in the same way it used to. Sometimes we'll see a person have a fever for a few days, and we treat that fever for the comfort of it. At this time the only treatment for the fever is Tylenol. Antibiotics aren't justified at this time as this fever is due to the dying process, not an infection.

Tylenol (suppositories) for the fever and a cool washcloth to the forehead and other comfort measures are recommended. If someone is hot we want to cool them down. Remove some of the covers, heavy pajamas or clothing, and take off their socks. We lose a lot of heat from the top of our head, and our feet, and this will cool them down faster.

Then if the person is having chills, we'll do this in

reverse and put more clothing or bedding on them. Some days you're adding and removing clothing and covers several times.

The Last Breath

Most of the time there's little to no drama when somebody dies, unlike TV and film portrayals. People experience breathing changes that are expected. Their color changes. Then the breathing simply stops. There may be a long sigh.

And that's it. They are gone.

Dying Alone

MOST FAMILIES DON'T WANT their loved one member to die alone. That's understandable, but there may be an issue with that.

Your loved one *may need to be alone* to let go.

Many, many times families have told me they'd had a vigil at the bedside for days and days, then they walked out of the room to get a cup of coffee, and the patient died in those 2 minutes!

This can be upsetting to family members, but it doesn't have to be.

Remember: The patient needed it. It's part of their process.

Think about it as a last gift from your loved one that you didn't see them take their last breath. That may be hard to hear, but what you're feeling about not being there is *your needs*. What *your loved one needed* was just that little bit of privacy to let go.

People who have more uptight or controlling personalities often do this. People who are very private or modest also need just a little private space to let go.

What you can do if your loved one is lingering is sit outside the room, check on them frequently, but give them some space. When you go in the room don't touch them or try to engage them. Just observe with your eyes and your heart. You know what's going on. (And so do they.) You don't need any further validation about the situation, so let them stay in their process without disruption that can pull them out of their process, making it go on longer than it has to.

After Someone Dies...Then What?

You, as the PCG, need to notify hospice that you think your loved one has passed away.

Call your hospice no matter what time of the day or night it is.

A nurse needs to come do the assessment as soon as possible to identify that the patient has indeed passed away.

The nurse will walk you through what happens next, from calling the funeral home, to medication disposal, to picking up of the equipment.

Calling the funeral home or mortuary: this the next step and the nurse will do that, but the nurse needs to know which one to call. If you wish to still have time with your loved one, the mortuary transfer can be delayed for a few hours, especially if someone is coming from out of town. If your loved one is in a nursing home or assisted living facility, they have different rules and will likely want to have the mortuary transfer occur quickly.

It is strongly recommended that you make funeral arrangements ahead of time. It's much easier if you can make those decisions prior to your death so family members aren't deciding things in a crisis or getting into arguments with family members who want to do something different.

Ideally if you can make the arrangements ahead of time, or at bare minimum, let your family members know what your desires are.

The mortuary will come pick up your loved one no matter what time of the day or night it is. They, like hospice, are a 24-hour service.

From the time the nurse calls, they will usually arrive to the home within 1 to 2 hours, depending on your location, rural or city, and whether they're out on another call. They usually drive a mini-van or SUV outfitted for their stretchers.

The mortuary will not do anything to your loved one immediately, just transfer to the mortuary. Then, they will contact the primary caregiver, or the contact person, to go over what type of service is desired and give them information that is needed for their processes.

Death Certificates

Death certificates come directly from the mortuary.

You'll order these documents at the time you're going over final arrangements with the mortuary. It is much easier and cheaper to get them at the time of death, rather than try to get additional copies later from the state. (There's Red Tape. Lots and lots of Red Tape.)

Generally large entities like Medicare, Medicaid, Social Security, banks, etc, will want their own *certified* copy of the death certificate. Other places, such as utility companies, may take a photocopy of a certificate for proof of death.

You have a limited timeframe to get this information to the above services. Mortuaries usually have a list of who you need to provide the death certificates to. Just ask for it.

Signs From Beyond

How do you know if your loved one made it to the other side and if they're okay? There are many stories about people who see their dead loved ones in the kitchen, or their bedroom, or walking down the hall in the home they used to live in.

Rest assured you are not losing your marbles or going crazy if you see these things. The signs are there if you are open to seeing them.

There's a beautiful video on YouTube about this. I'll include a link to the long version called: Send Me A Cardinal . Short version is here. They are about two sisters whose elderly mother told them that she would send a sign in the form of a cardinal that she had made it, and everything was fine. If you have the paperback or audiobook, go to YouTube and search: Send Me A Cardinal, and you'll find the videos.

The videos are about the two sisters figuring out that their mother had indeed sent them a sign in the form of a cardinal. Beautiful story.

Personal Story: My Dad

MY FATHER DIED in Pennsylvania at the end of October about 10 years ago. Before he died, my mom asked him to send her a sign that he'd made it and everything was fine.

Approximately 2 weeks after his death she had gone somewhere and when she returned to the house, she parked her car under the carport as usual. When she got out of the car, she saw her Clematis vine blooming as huge is a dinner plate!

At first she really didn't think much about it except that Dad had tried to weed-whack the vine off and ripped it out many times thinking it was a weed.

Let me tell you *nothing blooms in Pennsylvania in November*. Nothing. So my mom had her sign. She was satisfied with what she believed my father had sent to her.

Over the years, she's told me she has smelled cigarette smoke in the house. My dad was a lifelong smoker. He was also a bit of a trickster.

Approximately 3 months after my dad died in Pennsylvania, I believe he visited me in Albuquerque, NM. I was sitting in my living room watching TV. The TV stopped responding to the remote and then it went off by itself and would not come back on. I sat for a moment, trying to decide what to do, I started to smell cigarette smoke, very strongly.

There was nowhere for it to have come from in my house and my neighbors are too far away for it to have come from them.

At that moment, I had strong thoughts of my dad. So, I said out loud, "Hey Dad, if that's you, how about fixing my TV?"

My dad had been an *electronics repairman*, so it was reasonable of me to ask this. Within 2 minutes my TV came on by itself and never did it again.

Had my dad visited me? It's certainly something to think about. (I say yes.)

BRENDA HAMPTON, RN

Personal Story: My Aunt

A few years after my dad's death, my mother's sister died in Pennsylvania. She had also been a life-long smoker.

I was again sitting in my living room, and since it was a beautiful May day in Albuquerque, I had the inside front door open and outer security door locked, so I could catch the breeze.

It felt like someone came up behind me and blew cigarette smoke in my ear.

It was so strong that I turned around to see if there was somebody standing in my door smoking, but there was no one there. I called my mom and told her I believed Aunt Jane had just blown through town on her way to the other side and said goodbye to me.

Hearing that made my mom feel good, too.

You're free to have the opinion that what I've said about signs is a bunch of nonsense with unsubstantiated stories, just as I am free to tell the stories. They are experiences I've witnessed first-hand, and they're experiences patients, or their families, have told me about.

Feel free to believe or not believe, but I believe the spirits are present, that they come and go visiting us long after they have changed from physical form.

Energy is never destroyed. We are energy in physical form. What I believe is that our energy spirit is still present, simply in a different form.

People Know They Are Dying

OVER THE YEARS there have been times when families have asked us as hospice workers not to mention the word

166

hospice or tell the patient that they're dying. Some families have even asked us to remove our badges that contain the word *hospice*.

That's offensive to us whose careers are in hospice, and we've spent decades serving the needs of the dying. Please don't ask a hospice team member to remove their badges.

Asking hospice staff to hide our identities and not give the patient our best because the family is uncomfortable with the word hospice is a deceptive practice. I can't tell you how many times I've gone to visit a patient, and the family has asked me not to tell the patient she's dying. Then I go into the patient's room to talk to her, and she asks me not to tell the family she's dying!

Seriously.

People know they're dying. Many people have a sense they're dying many months ahead of time. Some people even know the day they will die.

Patient Story: I'm Going To Die Tonight

When I was an ICU nurse on my first travel nurse assignment in Florida, we had an elderly woman come in who had had a heart attack. She was in the ICU overnight and she told her nurse that she needed to talk to her son *that night* because she said she was going to die *that night*. Everyone kind of put that off to dementia, or confusion, but she was very insistent. Her nurse tried for several times to call him, but it was busy for hours.

This was back in the day when you could call the operator to break in on the conversation. The nurse was finally able to get the son on the phone and insistence of his mother, he came in to visit her that night. He came into the ICU and talked with his mother and before morning she died in her sleep. I don't know how, but she knew.

Personal Story: My Brother

My younger brother died in 2023 at age 55.

He was a severe diabetic. He lost both of his kidneys 10 years before his death, and he received a very generous kidney donation from a private donor. His own doctor wouldn't put him on the transplant list because of was the great chance that his diabetes would also destroy a transplanted kidney.

My brother got 10 more years of life after the transplant but was on all kinds of potent medications to prevent his body from rejection the kidney, though it was a perfect match.

Approximately one month before he died, he told our mother that he didn't think he was going to live much longer. She asked him why he thought that, but he wouldn't elaborate, he just said he had a feeling.

A month later he had a massive stroke. It was centered in the base of his brain. When the brain stem is gone, there's no survival without being permanently attached to machines.

He had an interesting experience about 10 months prior to his death. He was helping a woman he didn't know at the store he worked at, and she asked him if he knew anybody by the names of *Doris and Ed*. He said, "Yes, that's my aunt and uncle, but they're deceased." The lady said, "Yes, I know, but they're here in the room with you."

To say he was shocked was an understatement. He was not a believer in spirituality or religion at all. But this aunt and uncle were probably the relatives that he was the closest to as a child. They were waiting in the wings for him 10 months ahead of time though he hadn't known it until then. I don't know if he really believed it or not.

Very interesting topic to think of.

Patient Story: Picking A Day To Die

My first hospice patient was an elderly woman who lived alone. Her poodle was her only companion. He spent a lot of time in her bed with her. When I came to visit her, I had to go through the dog to get to her. They were fast companions, and he eventually became comfortable with me touching her.

One thing she said early in her hospice journey which started in January of that year was that she thought Good Friday would be a good day to die.

And yes, she died on Good Friday.

I am not kidding.

The most fascinating thing was that during the last week of her life her little poodle, who had been so attached to her, emotionally disengaged from her. He knew his owner was dying.

Animals know so much more than we do. They can see and sense things in ways that we can't. I don't know if they can smell chemical changes in the body and they understand what that is, or if it's on a spiritual level that they get the message. Either way, they understand something has changed.

A Word About Animals

Animals do experience grief at the loss of their owner. I recall reading a story about gentleman who left on a train to go get treatment somewhere and he died, his dog was left behind. It was a larger dog, and this dog would walk everyday to the train station and wait for his own for something like 5 years. He never got over that the loss of his human.

Many nursing facilities and assisted living have either a house dog or cat as a pet for all of the people in their facility.

There are many studies that people are more comfortable, happier, and live longer when there is an animal involved in their life, so it's understandable why so many care homes have animals.

I read about a cat named Oscar living in a nursing and rehab center in Rhode Island who would sleep with a certain resident for a couple of days and then that resident passed away. Here's a

It's like Oscar knew what was going on and was there to comfort the residents as they were dying.

Animals will often grieve for days, to weeks, after the death of their human. They need extra comfort and extra loving in this time to give them the support they need to do their grieving, and then they usually come out of it.

I took care of an older woman who asked that her dog be euthanized when she died if she died before her dog. Her daughter couldn't do it.

The dog wasn't ill. It wasn't in bad shape, and so she ended up keeping the dog. I think that was a better outcome for both the daughter and the dog.

When there are patients who have dogs on the bed with them, the family needs to take the dog out of the room for the nurse visit. That's advisable during routine nurse visits, as well as during the pronouncement of death.

Animals are often very protective of their owners. It's

safer for the nurse if the animal is moved out of the room for the nurse's assessment and then the animal can be put back in the bed to stay with their human until the mortuary arrives.

Patient Story: A Man And His Cat

A friend and hospice nurse told me the story of a patient that was in her care at one time. He was hanging on and suffering. He was surrounded by friends but had never married and had no children.

After several days of this, my friend said something just clicked with her. She leaned close to his ear and said, "I will take care of your cat."

He died fifteen minutes later.

Yes, animals are that important to some people. So important that they won't die unless they are reassured that their animal(s) will be taken care of.

Woo Woo Stuff at End-Of-Life

Brace yourself. This is a section you might not believe right now from your vantage point. I'm not trying to persuade you to believe in what can only be described as unbelievable.

What I'm going to share are things I've experienced directly and experiences that have been shared with me by hospice patients and their family members.

Hospice workers aren't generally psychic, but we do develop a sense, or intuition, of when someone is going to pass away. That's learned from reading the signs given by a patient's body, their vital signs, things they have said, and their behavior. We put it all together and give our best guess-timate.

There is more control over dying than you may think.

Mostly, we believe we have no control over the dying process, but that couldn't be further from the truth.

Have you ever heard of someone who said they were going to die on a certain date and then they did? That's not by coincidence.

Remember when I earlier referred to the patient who was in the ICU I worked at in Florida? Well, she wasn't the only one who knew when she was going to die.

Many patients hang on until a certain date, or die before a certain date, or even on their birthdays! Some people don't want to die on a holiday so it's not always a reminder to their families about the day they died.

Sometimes people will wait for a family member or friend to arrive, though they are in a coma, and then they will die when the person gets to their bedside.

When people are close to a grandchild or child who is in the military and stationed far away, hospice will assist in providing documents needed to get that person to the bedside of their loved one so both of them can have a last goodbye. People will hang on for that.

Patient Story: The Joker

One patient I took care of was also hanging on much longer than the family expected. All his end-of-life business had been taken care of and there was nothing they could identify that would keep him lingering.

He finally passed a few minutes after midnight, and I was present when he took his last breath. Just as I was about to start my talk about what happens next, one of the family members burst out laughing.

Of course, everyone looked at her to find out why she was laughing at such a somber moment.

She said, "It's April Fool's Day!" Then everyone else laughed. Apparently, the patient had been quite the joker, and it was in keeping with his personality to wait until April Fool's Day to die.

What an awesome last gift he gave to his family.

Founding Fathers: An Interesting Story

I'm referring to Thomas Jefferson and John Adams.

No, I'm not old enough to have taken care of these two men, but their death stories should go here.

A more famous rivalry in life and death is one you may or may not be aware of, and that was between Thomas Jefferson and John Adams, two of our Founding Fathers.

We in the USA know the famous date of July 4, 1776 was the day this nation secured its freedom. What is not commonly known is that many years later Thomas Jefferson died in Virginia, USA and John Adams died in Massachusetts, USA on the same date: July 4th!

That day was the 50th anniversary of the adoption of the US Constitution.

What also is not widely known is that exactly to the day, five years later, after these two deaths, former president James Monroe also died on July 4th, in 1831. There's an excellent article about all three deaths here.

A Word Of Thanks

CHAPTER 44

REFERENCES AND RESOURCES

H ere is a short list of documents and resources that you might find helpful.

Disclaimer: I don't get any kickbacks or benefit of any kind from these articles. They are helpful resources I wanted to include in this book. If they don't work for you, please feel free to do your own search.

How to find a hospice in your area: Search here

Grief support through hospice: Click Here

PPS Scale- Palliative Performance Scale

FAST Scale for Dementia: Functional Assessment Screening Tool

Free DPOA Form- https://freeforms.com/poa/durable/

Theft of Narcotics at End-Of-Life: Click Here

HIRING AN IN-HOME CAREGIVER:

A Place For Mom-Click Here.

How To Hire A Caregiver-AARP.

Getting Paid To Care For A Family Member-USA.gov.

Answer to question: what is the number 1 cause of

preventable death in the United States. Here's a link to the top 5 causes.

Medicare won't pay for hospital acquired infections any longer. Article here.

Morbidity and Mortality Weekly Report: Here.

Signs Your Loved One Is Visiting: Click Here.

Sisters and Cardinal: Short Version.

Sisters and Cardinal: Long Version.

Clematis vine images: Click Here.

Oscar the Cat: Click Here.

Grief in Animals: Click Here.

Presidential Deaths on July 4th: Click Here.

CHAPTER 45

STAY IN TOUCH

I f you have questions or would like information about booking Brenda for a speaking event, please contact her at:
Hospiceplainandsimple@gmail.com
Coming soon: hospiceplainandsimple.com

www.ingramcontent.com/pod-product-compliance
Lightning Source LLC
LaVergne TN
LVHW020054090426
835513LV00030B/2175